AIR WAR ARCHIVE

COMBAT OVER THE MEDITERRANEAN

THE RAF IN ACTION AGAINST THE GERMANS AND ITALIANS THROUGH RARE ARCHIVE PHOTOGRAPHS

AIR WAR ARCHIVE

COMBAT OVER THE MEDITERRANEAN

THE RAF IN ACTION AGAINST THE GERMANS AND ITALIANS THROUGH RARE ARCHIVE PHOTOGRAPHS

CHRIS GOSS

FRONTLINE
BOOKS

COMBAT OVER THE MEDITERRANEAN
The RAF In Action Against the Germans and Italians Through Rare Archive Photographs

First published in Great Britain in 2017
by Frontline Books
An imprint of Pen & Sword Books Limited,
47 Church Street, Barnsley,
South Yorkshire, S70 2AS.

ISBN 978-1-47388-943-9

A CIP catalogue record for this book is
available from the British Library

Typeset in 9.5/12pt Avenir
by Aura Technology and Software Services, India

Printed and bound in Great Britain
by CPI Group (UK) Ltd, Croydon, CR0 4YY

Pen & Sword Books Limited incorporates the imprints of Atlas,
Archaeology, Aviation, Discovery, Family History, Fiction, History, Maritime, Military, Military Classics,
Politics, Select, Transport, True Crime, Air World, Frontline Publishing, Leo Cooper, Remember When,
Seaforth Publishing,
The Praetorian Press, Wharncliffe Local History, Wharncliffe Transport,
Wharncliffe True Crime and White Owl.

For a complete list of Pen & Sword titles please contact
PEN & SWORD BOOKS LIMITED
47 Church Street, Barnsley, South Yorkshire, S70 2AS, United Kingdom
E-mail: enquiries@pen-and-sword.co.uk
Website: www.pen-and-sword.co.uk

CONTENTS

V

PREFACE

Dennis Ormonde Butler was born in Willesden, Middlesex on 19 July 1915. After his schooling he joined the RAF, being commissioned as an Acting Pilot Officer on 9 March 1936 and given the service number 37790. Dennis would spend most of the Second World War in the Mediterranean theatre and, unusually, commanded the same squadron, 252 Squadron, twice. He was awarded the Distinguished Flying Cross for his leadership on 21 November 1944. Dennis remained in the RAF after the war, eventually retiring as a Wing Commander on 3 February 1958.

I was fortunate to be introduced to 'DOB', as he was known by fellow Welshman Ray Morris, a former member of 252 Squadron's ground crew, and visited him a number of times at his home. Sadly, DOB passed away in 2005; Ray in 2016.

After Dennis' death I was asked by his son if I could help sort out his paperwork. It was during this process that I came across a remarkable collection of camera gun stills which had survived from DOB's time with 252 Squadron. His family generously presented me with this fascinating archive, and it is this that forms the basis of this book.

Whilst the photographs alone are of much interest, they all are dated and extremely clear. This information, and the relevant entries in the Form 540 Operations Record Book, help bring the pictures to life, so much so that at times the reader is almost given the impression he is in the cockpit. Consequently, the images in the pages that follow provide a unique insight into the air war over the Mediterranean and Aegean between 1942 and 1945.

This book is therefore dedicated to both DOB and Ray, as well as those, irrespective of nationality, who died or suffered in this theatre of operations during the Second World War.

Chris Goss,
Marlow, 2017.

ACKNOWLEDGEMENTS

I would like to thank the following for their assistance in compiling this book: Robert Forsyth, Bernd Rauchbach, Gianandrea Bussi, Andy Thomas, and Byron Tesapsides.

INTRODUCTION

It was at the start of June 1918 that 252 Squadron was formed at Tynemouth from Nos. 495, 507, 508, 509 and 510 flights. Initially equipped with the Airco DH6 and Short 184 seaplane, it carried out daylight coastal patrols over the North Sea. After a relatively uneventful war, during which time it also operated from Cramlington, Seaton Carew and Redcar, the squadron was run down, being finally disbanded on 30 June 1919.

On 21 November 1940, 252 Squadron was reformed at RAF Bircham Newton. From 1 December 1940, it was commanded by Squadron Leader Robert Yaxley MC, the Military Cross being awarded for his service with 2 Armoured Car Company in Palestine in November 1936.

At around the time that Yaxley took command, the squadron was in the process of moving to RAF Chivenor in Devon where it began to receive the Bristol Blenheim IF and IVF in preparation for being equipped with the Bristol Beaufighter. Deliveries of the Beaufighter were slow, as was day and night conversion training, but by the end of March 1941, the squadron was declared operational. At the start of April 1941, it moved to RAF Aldergrove in Northern Ireland from where it flew its first operational sortie, a fighter patrol over the Irish Sea, on 6 April 1941.

The squadron's first success came ten days later. The pilot involved was Flight Lieutenant Bill Riley. A very experienced fighter pilot, Riley had joined the RAF in 1935. He flew Gloster Gladiators with 263 Squadron over Norway in 1940, shooting down two Heinkel He 111s. He then flew Hurricanes with Nos. 145 and 302 squadrons in the Battle of Britain, during which he claimed a Junkers Ju 88 and a Messerschmitt Bf 109 destroyed and two Ju 88s and a Ju 87 probably destroyed.

In early 1941, Riley was posted to 252 Squadron. On 16 April 1941, he claimed the squadron's first kill when he shot down a Focke-Wulf Fw 200C-3 Condor at 14.20 hours. The latter, flown by Oberleutnant Hermann Richter of 1 *Staffel./Kampfgeschwader* 40, crashed off Blacksod Bay, North County Mayo. All of the German crew of six were reported missing. Riley had been flying with Warrant Officer George Donaldson, who had joined 252 Squadron in December 1940 and been awarded the Air Force Medal for his service in Afghanistan in 1928 and 1929.

Bill Riley's terse report detailing the engagement reads as follows: 'At the end of the patrol an enemy aircraft was sighted at 1420 hrs on a course of 210 degrees. Identified as a Condor. I started my attack from the beam quarter, finishing up astern. Fire was opened at 300 yards and continued in short bursts to point blank range when astern. The Condor replied with the midship gun. The Condor caught fire at the rear port wing root, both engines appearing unserviceable. The Condor swung to the left, straightened out, then dived into the sea in flames at an angle of 45 degrees. No survivors and very little wreckage were seen. The Condor was painted entirely green, with crosses silhouetted in white. No lower gondola observed.'

That same day, in fact just one hour and forty minutes later, 252 Squadron suffered its first loss in action. Whilst on a patrol off the Norwegian coast, operating from Sumburgh in the Shetland Islands, Flying Officer John Lane was shot down off Bergen by a Bf 110 flown by Oberleutnant Hans Kriegel of 7 *Staffel/Zerstörergeschwader* 76. Although he and Flight Sergeant Stan Cross were seen by the Germans to get out of the ditched Beaufighter, their bodies were never found. The Bf 110 was also damaged and the German pilot was wounded in the combat.

Nine days later, 252 Squadron was ordered to send fifteen aircraft to Luqa in Malta. This left seven aircraft and nine crews at Aldergrove under the command of Flight Lieutenant George Stockdale. The detachment left in UK continued to fly over the Irish Sea and North Atlantic before, on 14 June 1941, it formed the nucleus of 143 Squadron.

The 252 Squadron Malta detachment took off from RAF St Eval on 1 May 1941, thirteen aircraft arriving on 2 May 1941. During the journey one Beaufighter was forced to turn back and another landed in Portugal.

The squadron's role at Malta was to provide long-range fighter cover in addition to airfield strafing, but because of the German invasion of Greece and Crete, on 16 May 1941, nine aircraft were detached to Heraklion in Crete and the following day they strafed Hassani, Argos and Molai airfields claiming to have destroyed or damaged a number of aircraft for the loss of one Beaufighter.

In June 1941, the 252 Squadron detachment moved to Edku in Egypt where it operated together with 272 Squadron. At the end of that year, it began to reform as an independent squadron. By this time, Yaxley, having been promoted to Wing Commander, awarded the Distinguished Flying Cross in October 1941 and then the Distinguished Service Order in December 1941, was commanding 272 Squadron. He would take command of 117 Squadron the following year.

Yaxley was killed on 3 June 1943 when the passenger flight he was travelling on from Portreath to Gibraltar was shot down; all ten crew and passengers were reported missing. The victor was a Ju 88 C-6 of 15 *Staffel/Kampfgeschwader* 40 flown by *Leutnant* Heinz Olbrech. By this time, Yaxley had been promoted to Group Captain.

Command of 252 Squadron passed to Squadron Leader Arthur Wincott and it soon began flying independently from 272 Squadron. Aircraft would be detached back to Malta, but from 1942 onwards, 252 flew a plethora of attack missions, including shipping escort, shipping strikes and raids on Axis ground transport.

More air combat and ground strafing victories were achieved but at the same time, there was a steady loss of aircraft and crews. Indeed, 1942 would prove to be an intensive year. During September, for example, the crews flew a total of 201 sorties, a pattern that continued for the rest of the year.

September 1942 also saw Wing Commander Peter Bragg take command of 252 Squadron. He remained as CO until 6 December 1942 when he was shot down and captured during an airfield strafing attack. He was replaced by Wing Commander Patrick Ogilvie DSO, DFC, an experienced Bomber Command pilot whose arrival coincided both with the squadron's move to Berka and, at last, a reduction in its operational pace. (Patrick Ogilvie was reported missing 11 December 1944 after he had left the Squadron).

During the early months of 1943 the squadron carried out uneventful convoy escort duties, though from May 1943 onwards it began flying offensive sweeps of the Ionian Sea and Aegean, the aircraft now carrying bombs. Wing Commander Dennis Butler arrived in mid-May 1943.

As the Axis forces increasingly came under pressure and even began to retreat, very few enemy aircraft were encountered and when rockets were fitted to the Beaufighters in January 1944, attacks on enemy shipping then became the norm. By then, Canadian Wing Commander Patrick Woodruff DFC had taken command of the squadron (he was killed in an accident in Greece on

27 February 1945) but in March 1944, handed over to Wing Commander Bryce 'Willie' Meharg AFC. Meharg's time with the squadron was equally short as he was shot down and taken prisoner during an attack on a convoy off Crete on 1 June 1944. Unusually, Wing Commander Dennis Butler then returned to retake command.

For the remainder of 1944, the squadron carried out shipping strikes and even attacked land targets such as German garrisons. In February 1945, 252 Squadron was used against the Greek Communists, after when it carried out attacks against isolated German garrisons as well as air-sea rescue duties.

Wing Commander Butler then handed over to Squadron Leader Tony Hunter in March 1945 (he was killed in a car accident in Greece on 19 September 1945), before Squadron Leader Cosmo Price-Owen took over in April 1945. As the last images in this book will reveal, the squadron flew its final operational mission of the war on 5 May 1945, when it undertook rocket attacks against coastal gun positions on Melos.

Having been based at Hassani in Greece since February 1945, the squadron moved to what would be its last base at Araxos in August 1945. Wing Commander Kenneth Gray took command in May 1945, though by then flying was limited by serviceability and demobilisation.

In April 1946, Wing Commander Douglas Hayward DSO took command of a much depleted 252 Squadron, remaining with it until it was finally disbanded at Araxos on 1 December 1946.

BELOW: Beaufighter R2153 photographed during 1941. This aircraft survived its time on 252 Squadron and ended its days at 2 OTU.

An air-to-air shot of R2198. Having also been operated by 252 Squadron, this aircraft was transferred to 2 OTU, only to be written off in a crash at Driffield on 4 April 1942.

This is Beaufighter Ic T3237/PN-K at Aldergrove, circa 1941. This aircraft was flown by Flight Lieutenant Bill Riley on 16 April 1941 when he shot down a Focke-Wulf Fw 200. Probably still being used by Riley, T3237was written-off after being damaged by a Hurricane at Luqa, Malta, on 3 May 1941.

It was on 16 April 1941 that 252 Squadron suffered its first loss in action. Whilst on a patrol off the Norwegian coast Flying Officer John Lane was shot down off Bergen by a Messerschmitt Bf 110 flown by *Oberleutnant* Hans Kriegel of 7 *Staffel/ Zerstörergeschwader* 76 – who is seen here.

One of the Beaufighters lost whilst being operated by 252 Squadron. T4827/BT-R was reported missing on 28 June 1942.

LZ286/A photographed at Gambut, 14 July 1944. It was flown operationally the following day by Wing Commander Butler and Flying Officer Roland Kemp.

Beaufighters of 252 Squadron head out on a mission.

Ground crew working on one of 252 Squadron's Beaufighters, circa 1944.

Pilot Officer John Underwood in NT895/H, 21 September 1944.

Two members of 252 Squadron, unfortunately unnamed, in front of one of its Beaufighters.

An air-to-air shot of Beaufighter NE247/X taken in September 1944.

Warrant Officer J.S. Bates and Pilot Officer Frank Gresswell, September 1944.

Beaufighter NE373/A pictured at an unidentified airfield.

HOW   TO

WHEN IN AREA........ CANNON/ TO FIRE. /IGHT ACRO// AND /WITCHED ON — ZERO DEPRE//ION. /ET ALTIMETER TO HEIGHT ABOVE /EA LEVEL.	WHEN ORDERED, OPEN OUTWARD/ FROM LEADER AND CLIMB AT 160 KT/. 2400 R.P.M. AND +4 TO 6 BOO/T TO 2500 FEET.	AT 2500·FT. THROTTLE BACK TO −1 BOO/T AND REDUCE REV/ TO 2100. MAINTAING HEIGHT AND /TATION ON LEADER APPROACH TARGET WITH WEAVING EVA/IVE ACTION. /PEED NOT EXCEEDING 160 KT.

"ANTI - FLAK"

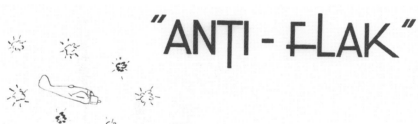

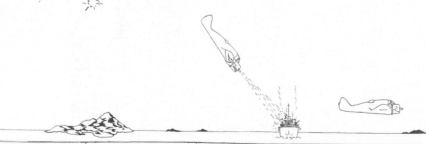

WHEN LEVEL AND TARGET I/ ABOUT TO DI/APPEAR BENEATH AIRCRAFT/ NO/E. THROTTLE **RIGHT BACK** AND NO/E OVER.	BY MEAN/ OF **GENTLE** CORRECTIVE ACTION. PLACE TARGET IN /IGHT ALLOWING DEFLECTION FOR **WIND** AND **TARGET TRAVEL.**	/ETTLE DOWN TO A /TEADY DIVE, OPEN FIRE AND **GIVE UNTIL IT HURT/** (150 RD/. PER GUN).	BREAK AT 500 FEET WITH WEAVING EVA/IVE ACTION OVER OR AROUND THE TARGET. CONTINUE ON /AME COUR/E A/ FOR ATTACK AND AWAIT ORDER/ FROM LEADER.

A pair of drawings, produced by 252 Squadron, that provided guidance for new crews.

Squadron Leader Keith Faulkner DFC can be seen on the left in this image.

Squadron Leader Keith Faulkner DFC poses with 252 Squadron groundcrew under 'Q'.

Beaufighters of 252 Squadron flying low over the water.

The individual on the right, probably pictured on NV373/A, is Dennis Butler.

Three 252 Squadron Beaufighters in the air on 21 September 1944. Nearest the camera is NT895/H with Pilot Officer John Underwood at the controls.

Some of 252 Squadron's Beaufighters pictured flying over the Royal Palace in Athens on 8 May 1945. In the foreground is NV248/S, whilst NV381/P can be seen beyond.

Another photograph of 252 Squadron over Athens on 8 May 1945. On the right is NV259/Y.

Part I
1942

WEDNESDAY, 7 OCTOBER 1942

On 6 October 1942, a force of six Beaufighters of 252 Squadron, led by Wing Commander Peter Bragg, carried out a strafing attack against the Italian seaplane base at Bomba in Menelao Bay, Libya. The crews involved claimed to have damaged seven Cant. Z.506 seaplanes, the latter probably from 148a *Squadriglia Regia Marina*.

The following day, four Beaufighters of 252 Squadron, this time led by Flying Officer Ian 'Nipper' Maclean and Sergeant Ernest Strange in Beaufighter T5052, lifted off from Edku in Egypt at 12.50 hours to carry out a repeat of the attack. It is this sortie that features in the following set of pictures.

On the 7th the RAF pilots claimed to have damaged five Cant Z.506 seaplanes. They then claimed to have damaged an F-boat and, in the Gazala area, strafed two lorries and trailers which they destroyed – as well as a further lorry full of troops. Finally, they attacked five tented camps, subsequently reporting that they had caused at least fifty casualties.

The first photograph, (1), shows two of the four Beaufighters of their way to the target on 7 October 1942. The next pair of images, (2) and (3), are of two Beaufighters strafing a mixture of Cant Z.501s and Z.506s in Menelao Bay. The next three photographs, (4), (5) and (6) respectively, show what appears to be Italian vehicles being strafed, whilst the final one, (7), was taken whilst on of the tented camps was under attack.

All four Beaufighters landed safely at 17.15 hours, although T5114, the aircraft flown by Sergeant G. Nettleship and Warrant Officer J.B. Blake, was damaged by Flak.

MONDAY, 12 OCTOBER 1942

At 13.40 hours on 12 October 1942, Flying Officer Charles McMills, a Canadian, and Sergeant H. Bicknell were at the controls of Beaufighter T5110 of 252 Squadron, when they led another three Beaufighters which were escorting Bristol Bisley bombers tasked to attack a train.

The train was not located so the Beaufighters went looking for other targets, during which they claimed to have destroyed a Junkers Ju 52, damaged a Messerschmitt Bf 110 and a two-masted schooner. They also destroyed several lorries and trailers and set thirteen railway trucks on fire. Photographs (8) and (9) graphically reveal one of the Beaufighters hitting the train. All four Beaufighters landed safely at 17.20 hours.

MONDAY, 19 OCTOBER 1942

A week later, on 19 October, a pair of 252 Squadron's Beaufighters took off at 12.15 hours to undertake a further strafing mission. The two aircraft were T4932, flown by Sergeant G. Nettleship and Flight Sergeant S.G. Deacon, and T5036, which was crewed by Pilot Officer R.B. Watson and Sergeant G.D. Hudson. A further two Beaufighters took off at the same time to strafe enemy road vehicles.

The first pair hit and destroyed a locomotive and left six wagons smoking. They then destroyed a petrol bower before landing at Edku at 14.45 hours. Images (10) and (11) were taken during this sortie.

Part II
1943

SUNDAY, 23 MAY 1943

Just before midday on 23 May 1943, three Beaufighters of 252 Squadron, led by Flight Lieutenant Keith Faulkner and navigator Flight Lieutenant Frank Quinn in Beaufighter EL757, took off from Magrun landing ground in Libya on an offensive sweep of the Ionian Sea. Though not much was seen, a two-masted schooner was attacked, though no damage was seen to have been inflicted. The camera gun footage – examples of which can be seen in photographs (1), (2) and (3) – shows how lucky the schooner and its crew were.

TUESDAY, 25 MAY 1943

On the afternoon of 17 May 1943, a formation of six Beaufighters of 252 Squadron, led by Squadron Leader Ernest Meads, tried to locate and attack the seaplane base at Preveza in north-western Greece. Bad weather, however, forced them to turn back.

The next attempt to locate and attack Preveza was made on the morning of 25 May 1943. On this occasion, seven Beaufighters took off from Bersis for the first stage of the flight to Magrun. It was from the latter that, at 13.15 hours, six of the Beaufighters lifted off for Preveza. Once again the formation was led by Ernest Meads whose navigator was Sergeant Geoff Goodes – they were flying Beaufighter X8144.

Arriving over the seaplane base at high speed and low level, fourteen enemy aircraft were spotted. These were a mix of Italian and German types and all, apart from Red Cross-marked Junkers Ju 52s, were attacked – illustrated by pictures (4), (5), (6) and (7). The six RAF fighters claimed to have destroyed a Cant Z.501 and two Cant Z.506s. A Cant Z.506 was probably destroyed, with five Cant Z.506s damaged and two Ju 52s damaged.

The units that these enemy aircraft belonged to are not known. The attackers also set fire to a petrol dump, the smoke from which rose to 1,000 feet, being visible thirty miles away. To add further insult to injury, on the way back they attacked a schooner, also setting this on fire, smoke from it rising to 300 feet – see image (8). All six Beaufighters had landed safely by 19.10 hours.

4

SUNDAY, 30 MAY 1943

Having arrived from RAF Ismalia on 11 May 1943, on the 30th of the same month it was the turn of the new Commanding Officer of 252 Squadron, Wing Commander Dennis 'DOB' Butler, to fly his first operational mission with his command. The task that morning was an offensive sweep by three Beaufighters, the small force being led by Dennis Butler, together with Flight Lieutenant Frank Quinn, in Beaufighter EL391.

During the sortie the Beaufighters located and then attacked a merchant ship which was loaded with a deck cargo of hay. By the time they turned for home, the ship was ablaze and grey smoke was observed rising to 150 feet. The victim on this occasion was the 1,046 ton *Tenacia Gennari*. Its crew managed to get the fire under control and, with the help of the tug *Littoria*, succeeded in making its destination of the Gulf of Patras. Note, in image (9), the hay forward and the crew's washing aft hanging from the masts.

FRIDAY, 11 JUNE 1943

On 11 June 1943, Wing Commander Dennis Butler, together with Flight Lieutenant Frank Quinn in Beaufighter EL391, led another two Beaufighters on an offensive sweep. They attacked a two-masted schooner of 100 tons, shooting away its stern sail, rudder and holing it above the waterline.

A second schooner of 175 tons was then attacked and the Beaufighters set the deck cargo on fire, the RAF crews noting black smoke rising to forty feet. Then they attacked a small steam coaster eight times, observing a bright flash on the stern, with the bridge, deck and aft superstructure left on fire. Finally, they attacked what appeared to be an abandoned schooner.

After a flight time of six hours and twenty-five minutes, Dennis Butler's Beaufighter was the second to land. This sequence of photographs, (10), (11), (12) and (13), was taken during the attack on the first schooner.

10

11

FRIDAY, 18 JUNE 1943

Another offensive sweep was carried out on 18 June 1943, but this time Beaufighter EL391 was flown by Squadron Leader David Pritchard.

Three Beaufighters got airborne from Bercis at 12.10 hours and attacked a two-masted schooner and then four small caiques, though without any visible result. All aircraft landed without incident at 17.25 hours.

The first photograph, (14), shows one of the formation during this mission whilst the second, (15), is Kyparissia Harbour and the ship *Agia Zone II*, which was stranded there on 11 February 1940 due to bad weather.

SUNDAY, 20 JUNE 1943

On the morning of 20 June 1943, Wing Commander Dennis Butler led three other Beaufighters from Magrun to Berka. He was flying his usual aircraft, EL391, and was crewed back with his usual navigator, Flight Lieutenant Frank Quinn.

An hour and forty minutes after arriving at Berka, the four aircraft took off on an offensive sweep. In Killini Harbour, they attacked a pair of two-masted schooners and two small caiques. Six 250lb bombs were dropped, after which eight attacks were made with cannon and machine-guns. Disappointingly, the only visible result was 'a small amount of dark brown smoke from one of the schooners'.

All four aircraft landed safely after a flying time of around five hours and twenty minutes. This series of images shows the attack on the harbour and the Beaufighters flying over Killini with apparent impunity. Pictures (16), (17), (18), (19) and (20) show bombs falling amongst the schooners and caiques; (21) shows the clouds of dust and smoke rising from the harbour and surrounding buildings; and (22) the water settling down after a number of explosions. Note, in (23), the lady in black watching the Beaufighters in the distance, unaware that another is taking photographs as it flies over her.

16

17

18

SUNDAY, 27 JUNE 1943

There was another very successful day for 252 Squadron exactly a week later on 27 June 1943. After flying from Magrun to Berka in the morning, four aircraft, led by Squadron Leader Eric Meads and Sergeant Geoff Goodes in JL521, took off to undertake an offensive sweep. This resulted in the Beaufighters attacking an Italian convoy of three merchant ships escorted by two auxiliary naval vessels in the Levkas Canal south of Preveza.

The RAF crews attacked what they reported was a large motor vessel of 6,000 tons; two aircraft claimed to have hit it, whilst the other two reported near misses. Their bombs had in fact hit the 3,779-ton *Quirinale* which was then beached at Santa Maura; the *Quirinale* would become the centre of attention for the RAF a week later. The *Qurinale* is visible in this photograph (24).

24

MONDAY, 28 JUNE 1943

For 252 Squadron, 28 June 1943 would be a red-letter day. At lunchtime, four aircraft led by Flight Lieutenant John Manley and Sergeant James King, in EL369, flew from Magrun to Berka. It was from the latter that they took off at 15.15 hours on an offensive sweep.

The formation came across a Cant Z.1007 of 190a *Squadrigila*, 35° *Stormo*. A subsequent report stated that, 'a Cant Z1007 twin tail aircraft was sighted and attacked by one of our aircraft; pieces were seen to disintegrate from the port wing and the enemy aircraft dived in the sea' – picture (25). *Teniente Pilot* Carmelo La Micela, *Sergente Pilot* Iacopo Cancellier, 1° *Aviere RT* Bruno Cosoli, 1° *Aviere Mot* Virginio Dilzeni and *Aviere Scelto Arm* Angelo Padua were all killed.

The four Beaufighters then headed to the west coast of Morea where they all attacked a steel bridge, dropping five bombs but with no results. One aircraft then fired on a train leaving it in a cloud of steam – pictures (26) and (27). Another Beaufighter dropped a bomb near the fourth wagon, whilst a third strafed the carriages. One aircraft attacked six wagons, claiming to have destroyed three, after which it attacked another train of six wagons. Finally, two aircraft attacked four wireless masts and a small tented encampment, though with no confirmed results.

25

WEDNESDAY, 30 JUNE 1943

At 06.00 hours on 30 June 1943, Baltimore AG801, coded T of 203 Squadron, took off from Berka III on a photo-reconnaissance sortie. The aircraft was crewed by Warrant Officer P.D. Carlton (Pilot), Flying Officer H.L. Lewis (Navigator) and Sergeant J.M. Gray and Sergeant F.C. Barton (Wireless Operator/Air Gunners).

The Baltimore landed back at base nearly six hours later having photographed the Levkas Canal, spotting dredgers and the beached *Quirinale*, images (28) and (29), which had been fatally damaged by 252 Squadron three days previously.

THURSDAY, 1 JULY 1943

At 06.25 hours on 1 July 1943, Squadron Leader David Pritchard and Flying Officer S.G. Harris, at the controls of EL406, and Flight Sergeant R.H. Robson and Sergeant G.E. Peckover, took off to carry out a further attack on the beached *Quirinale* in the Levkas Canal.

The first photograph, (30), shows one of the Beaufighters banking hard to port over *Quirinale* (bottom left); hits can be seen on her in the second photograph (31). By this stage, *Quirinale* was effectively sunk but still attracted the attention of the RAF as it was a perfect opportunity to permanently block the canal. Both 252 Squadron aircraft landed safely at 12.20 hours.

The presence of further shipping in and around the canal entrance prompted a further attack later that day by 227 Squadron.

At 11.30 hours on 1 July 1943, four Beaufighters of 227 Squadron, led by Flying Officer B.R.E. Amos and Sergeant W.H. Duncan in EL476/R, took off from El Magrun and also headed for the Levkas Canal. There where they carried out a low-level bombing and strafing run on a dredger.

Flying at fifty feet, the raiders approached their target at 14.10 hours. It was immediately noticed that *Quirinale* was listing 45 degrees to port in the centre of the canal entrance. A dredger of 250-300 tons was to her south, whilst 300 yards beyond that there was a second smaller dredger with two tugs nearby.

Flying Officer Amos attacked first, with the remaining three Beaufighters coming in from starboard. Cannon and machine-gun hits were recorded against both dredgers, after which Canadian Flying Officer C.B. Feight and Sergeant G.A. Brown, in EL239/N, strafed the larger dredger and released two bombs, both of which narrowly missed – image (32). Feight then noticed that machine-gun fire aimed at his formation leader was coming from the canal bank – he succeeded in silencing the gun with a short burst of fire.

Sergeant D.E. Warnes and Flying Officer J.W.D. Thomas in JL533/K then attacked, dropping two bombs which overshot by ten yards. It was then that the four aircraft came under machine-gun fire from the canal's west bank and light and medium anti-aircraft fire from the hillside and nearby town. So, at 14.27 hours, the Beaufighters turned for home.

However, 21-year-old Flight Sergeant John Hawkes-Reed and Warrant Officer L.R. De Maniel, who had been flying JL532/L, failed to return having fallen victim to the anti-aircraft fire. Hawkes-Reed was killed; De Maniel captured. Of the remaining Beaufighters, the aircraft flown by Sergeant Warnes was holed by 40mm gunfire which caused hydraulic failure and resulted in him crash-landing back at base.

FRIDAY, 2 JULY 1943

On 2 July, just two Beaufighters of 252 Squadron, EL391, flown by Wing Commander Dennis Butler, and EL369, with Canadian Flying Officer Frank Foyston at the controls, carried out an offensive sweep of the Ionian Sea.

During this sortie the pair attacked a schooner, picture (33), and bombed a steel bridge. The latter can be seen in images (34) and (35) – note the cannon fire and exploding bomb. The flight lasted five hours and forty-five minutes.

FRIDAY, 9 JULY 1943

The mission flown by 252 Squadron from Misurata on 9 July 1943 was quite uneventful, being that of escort duty for Convoy *Carbon*.

The first section of seven aircraft took off at 04.45 hours and landed back at 09.25 hours. A second section of four aircraft took off at 07.30 hours, in turn landing between 12.15 and 13.00 hours. A final section of two aircraft took off at 10.25 hours, returning at 15.25 hours.

The two photographs seen here, (36) and (37), were taken by Wing Commander Dennis Butler's navigator, Flight Lieutenant Frank Quinn, the pair, flying in EL530, leading the second section.

Carbon is believed to have been Convoy KMS.19. This consisted of forty-six merchant ships and two escorts which were destined for Operation *Husky*, the Allied invasion of Sicily. All aircraft later returned to Magrun.

36

SATURDAY, 10 JULY 1943

The day after having escorted Convoy *Carbon*, two of 252 Squadron's aircraft, those flown by Wing Commander Dennis Butler, EL530, and Flight Lieutenant John Manley, EL369, flew from Magrun to Berka. At 11.06 hours, the pair took off together with a Baltimore, AG917 of 203 Squadron which was crewed by Lieutenant Hugh Nottingham (Pilot), Sergeant Wilfred Donner (Navigator), Sergeant Arthur Oldham and Flight Sergeant Tony Roberts (Wireless Operator/Air Gunners), to attack shipping off south-west Crete, the exact position being 35 degrees 12 minutes North 23 degrees 41 minutes East.

On reaching what the Germans stated was Paloechora, picture (38), both Beaufighters attacked and hit an Italian patrol boat causing casualties, (39). At this point they were then subjected to intense medium and light anti-aircraft fire from the shore. Both Beaufighters were hit – as was the Baltimore which then caught fire. A single parachute was seen before the Baltimore plunged into the sea just off the shore. The lone survivor was the pilot who was captured badly wounded; such was the extent of his injuries that he died in hospital three days later. The bodies of the other three crew members were never recovered. Both Beaufighters then returned to Berka.

WEDNESDAY, 14 JULY 1943

Taken on 14 July 1943, picture (40) shows the Italian seaplane base at Preveza. Looking south, it was taken by Baltimore FA171/A of 203 Squadron, this being crewed by Flying Officer A.R. Tubbenhauer (Pilot), Flight Sergeant H.G. Hampton (Navigator), and Flight Sergeant R.D. Hoslick and W.S. Allen (Wireless Operator/Air Gunner).

Tubbenhauer had taken off from Berka at 06.28 hours on a reconnaissance mission, landing back at 11.39 hours. Thirteen seaplanes can been seen in this photograph. The identity of the Italian unit is not certain, but by the start of September 1943, 139a *Squadriglia* was based at Preveza and 184a *Squadriglia* at Pola Puntisella. It is believed that this mission was in preparation for an attack made on Preveza by 252 Squadron on 19 July 1943.

The spit of land in the centre of the inlet, where the waterway turns to the left, now carried a road that joins both banks. Much of the ground in this picture has been built on in the years since the war.

SATURDAY, 17 JULY 1943

On the morning of 17 July 1943, four aircraft of 252 Squadron, those flown by Flight Sergeant R.H. Robson (EL509), Sergeant Lewis Passow (EL228), Flight Sergeant D.G.R. 'Paddy' Ward (EL473) and Sergeant Harry Humphries (EL391), got airborne from Berka at 11.40 hours. The four crews were tasked with an offensive sweep.

In addition to strafing a train in Killini Harbour, they dropped bombs on a two-masted schooner, but missed. Taken during the attack, photographs (41) and (42) provide a vivid illustration of just how low the Beaufighters were – and how close one of them was to its target, only just missing its mast. It is not surprising, therefore, that one Beaufighter returned to Bersis with damage caused by hitting a tree top.

MONDAY, 19 JULY 1943

Five days after Baltimore FA171/A of 203 Squadron had taken its images of the enemy seaplane base at Preveza 252 Squadron was ordered to make its visit. Six aircraft flew from Magrun to Bersis at breakfast time and then at 10.15 hours took off on the raid. The formation was led by Wing Commander Dennis Butler in JL521. He was accompanied by Flight Lieutenant John Manley in EL569, Flight Lieutenant Harry Hubbard in V8335, Sergeant Lewis Passow in EL475, Flight Sergeant Paddy Ward in EL228 and Flight Sergeant R.H. Robson in EL281.

Two Cant Z.506s and a Cant Z.501 were claimed destroyed and three more seaplanes damaged. The Beaufighters then bombed the slipway and quarters as well as strafed anti-aircraft gun positions before heading for home. This remarkable set of photographs – (43), (44), (45) and (46) – are believed to have been taken by Dennis Butler's navigator, Flight Lieutenant Frank Quinn. Picture (43) shows the single Cant Z.501.

43

WEDNESDAY, 21 JULY 1943

When 203 Squadron's Flying Officer E.V. Cullen, and his crew of Sergeant L. Beacon (Navigator), Pilot Officer C.S. Pearce and Sergeant S.G. Ladbrooke (Wireless/Operator Air Gunners), returned to the Levkas Canal on the morning of 21 July 1943 on a photographic reconnaissance sortie, the stricken *Quirinale* was still there blocking the canal entrance.

Cullen was flying Baltimore AG803 and, as photograph (47) shows, he flew beyond the range of the anti-aircraft guns to get his shot, albeit there appears to be evidence of an exploding shell top right of the image. Note the absence of other shipping.

SATURDAY, 24 JULY 1943

On the morning of 24 July 1943, four aircraft from 252 Squadron flew from Magrun to Berka III, after which they took off on an anti-shipping strike. The Beaufighters involved were flown by Flight Sergeant Paddy Ward, who was in JL523, Flight Sergeant Desmond De Villiers in T5256, Sergeant Alexander McKeown in EL569 and Flying Officer F.A. Cohen in EL281.

For reasons not stated, the aircraft attacked the secondary target of Kalamata airfield. Several buildings were hit by bombs, the RAF crews noting that debris was thrown up into the air after which they strafed and set a truck on fire – events captured on film in (48), (49) and (50). All aircraft had landed safely by 16.25 hours.

TUESDAY, 27 JULY 1943

Judging by the photographic evidence that has survived to this day, the afternoon of 27 July 1943 must have been quite a spectacular one for the crews of 252 Squadron – though little detail is provided in the Operations Record Book.

Just after lunchtime three aircraft flew from Magrun to Bercis – these being Flight Lieutenant Keith Faulkner in JL521, Sergeant Donald Pearson in EL475 and Sergeant George Hobdell in EL281. An hour and a half later the trio took off on yet another Ionian Sea offensive sweep.

In the course of the sortie the three crews claimed to have beached or sunk three caiques and damaged two more with gunfire before strafing an armed trawler, hitting it on the superstructure. The first three photographs, (51), (52) and (53), were taken during the attacks on the caiques, whilst the last two, (54) and (55), show the trawler being hit. The location is Vathi on the island of Meganissi.

THURSDAY, 5 AUGUST 1943

The first 252 Squadron offensive mission of August 1943 came on the afternoon of the fifth of the month when Wing Commander Dennis Butler, in JL521, and Flight Sergeant Paddy Ward, in JL523, went on an offensive sweep, ending up attacking Preveza and shipping in the harbour – (56), (57) and (58).

The two Beaufighters strafed a trawler killing a gunner. Butler's bombs overshot and exploded on the quayside, whilst Ward's bombs landed amongst three schooners but failed to explode. After this, he strafed warehouses in the town. From the photographs, it would appear that the Italian seaplanes had moved elsewhere. The flight lasted five hours, with both aircraft back on the ground by 19.30 hours.

SATURDAY, 7 AUGUST 1943

Two offensive sweeps were conducted by two aircraft each on 7 August 1943. The first pair to get airborne, Sergeant Lewis Passow in EL473 and Flight Sergeant Norman Creswell in EL598, operated against shipping in the Ionian Sea with. Airborne at midday, they happened across a 1,000-ton coaster, (59) and (60), which was strafed and bombed – only for all of the bombs failing to explode.

German records state: 'It is reported that an enemy air attack with bombs and gunfire was made on an Italian submarine chaser on the afternoon of 7 August in the Peloponese area, exact position unspecified. The submarine chaser was slightly damaged. One plane was set on fire by gunfire.' Despite the fact remark, both Beaufighters landed safely at 17.45 hours with no reports of damage.

SUNDAY, 8 AUGUST 1943

During the afternoon of 8 August 1943, a pair of 252 Squadron's Beaufighters, namely EL473, flown by Flight Lieutenant Harry Hubbard, and EL475, Flying Officer G. Westinghouse, attacked what was described as a 'corvette type vessel' with bombs and gunfire at Gythion – captured in (61) and (62). Two bombs overshot whilst the third exploded alongside the warship on the quay. When they left, smoke was rising from the ship to fifty feet.

The pair then attacked a two-masted schooner with the remaining bomb which overshot but failed to explode. A further four schooners were then strafed before the two Beaufighters landed safely after a flight of five hours. German records record the following: 'Two enemy planes attacked the harbor and the Italian battery *Cython* [*sic*] in the Southern Peloponese on the afternoon of 8 August. A small naval vessel was sunk.' Another report states that the two aircraft attacked at 15.30 hours, during which a small Italian warship was sunk with two killed and one wounded.

61

SUNDAY, 15 AUGUST 1943

There was another day of activity off the west coast of Greece a week later on 15 August 1943. Two aircraft, JL509 flown by Flight Lieutenant Keith Faulkner and EL473 with Flight Sergeant George Hobdell at the contraols, were on an offensive reconnaissance when they spotted and attacked two 3,000-ton freighters – (62) and (63). Two bombs overshot and failed to explode on the first vessels, whilst the following two bombs fell between the ships and failed to explode. Faulkner and Hobdell also managed to strafe a 200-ton schooner, (64), and avoid a Flak position on the top of a hill, (65), as they headed off, landing safely at 16.50 hours. German records state that ships off Preveza were subjected to low-level bombing and strafing attack.

MONDAY, 16 AUGUST 1943

Early in the afternoon of 16 August 1943, four Bristol Beaufighters of 603 Squadron lifted off from their airfield at Berka III and headed for Missolonghi in western Greece. The four were led by former Battle of Britain pilot Squadron Leader George Atkinson in EL831/A, his navigator being Sergeant Emeric Wimberger. Their target that afternoon was enemy shipping in the harbour, the biggest vessel there being the 3,000-tonne Italian freighter *Livensa*.

At 16.38 hours, the four Beaufighters approached the target at low level and high speed. A direct hit and two near misses by 250lb bombs were reported on *Livensa* which was also subjected to cannon and machine-gun fire, as was another smaller ship of about 1,500 tonnes.

The first photograph, (66), shows, to the right, a Beaufighter (circled) attacking the smaller ship with gunfire. In picture (67) the same Beaufighter can be seen breaking away to starboard whilst another Beaufighter is seen near the bows of *Livensa*. The next image in the set, (68), shows a Beaufighter pulling up over *Livensa* before the aircraft from which the photographs were taken is seen flying through its masts, (69) – note the bullet holes in the smoke stack. The final picture, (70), is the view looking back towards the harbour and the Beaufighter's delayed-action bombs exploding.

Having also attacked anti-aircraft positions, the Beaufighters landed back at Berka, undamaged, early that evening. German records indicate that an Italian steamer was damaged and another ship sunk at Missolonghi during air attacks on the night of 15 and afternoon of 16 August 1943. The crews of the other Beaufighters were Flying Officer A. Honig DFM and Sergeant R.G. Finlay in EL523/C, Flight Sergeant C.B. Megone and Sergeant J.E. Williams in JL625/R, and Sergeant J.P. Hey and Sergeant E.H. Worrall in JL537/M.

66

TUESDAY, 17 AUGUST 1943

During an attack on a ship in Zante Harbour on 17 August 1943, one of two bombs dropped by the 252 Squadron Beaufighter flown by Sergeant Donald Pearson, EL228, exploded on the jetty, the other between the quay and the target ship, (71). The second Beaufighter, V8347 flown by Sergeant Alexander McKeown, was forced to take evasive action due to heavy anti-aircraft fire.

    The bell tower and large structure that dominate this view is Saint Dionysios Church, also known as St Dennis Church, which is one of the most recognizable buildings as you enter the harbour today.

WEDNESDAY, 18 AUGUST 1943

During another Ionian Sea offensive reconnaissance on 18 August 1943, three caiques at anchor were attacked with bombs and gunfire, albeit without result – smoke from the attack can just be made out in (72). The two pilots involved, Wing Commander Dennis Butler in EL473 and Flight Sergeant Harry Humphries in V8347, then targeted a 500-ton coaster, (73), which was hit on the stern with one bomb and then strafed with the bridge being hit, (74). German records state the attack occurred in Vonitsa Bay off Preveza.

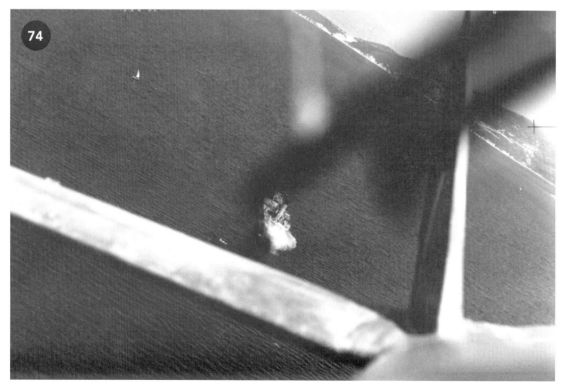

THURSDAY, 19 AUGUST 1943

On 19 August, 603 Squadron sent a detachment of Beaufighters to 252 Squadron's base at Berka III and then, at 14.10 hours, took off to attack shipping at Missolonghi. They were approaching the target area at 16.34 hours when they spotted warning flares rising to 2,000 feet from Cape Skinari and Cape Killini.

Despite the fact that the defenders had been alerted, the Beaufighters attacked a 2,000-ton ship in the harbour at 17.02 hours. Squadron Leader Herbert Laycock and Sergeant Robert Scott, in JL539/T, who were leading the formation, hit the ship with gunfire forward of the bridge. This was the cue for Flight Sergeant P.H. Miller and Flight Sergeant R. Everett, in X8105/T, and Flying Officer H.H. Giles and Sergeant L. Coulstock, in JL504/H, to make their attack. Each aircraft dropped two 250lb bombs which undershot. The remaining Beaufighter involved in the sortie was V8321/V flown by Flight Sergeant W.A. Eacott and Flight Sergeant W. Pritchard.

At that moment the starboard engine of Laycock's Beaufighter was seen to catch fire and he immediately force-landed beside a road north-west of the town – which these two photographs, (75) and (76), show. JL539 then burst into flames. Although both men survived, they were badly burned and were later reported to have died on 26 August 1943. Herbert Laycock had flown Hurricanes with 79 and 87 squadrons in the Battle of Britain before moving to 603 Squadron in 1943.

The remaining three Beaufighters then spotted other shipping but did not attack. They landed back at Berka III at 19.45 hours.

75

SATURDAY, 21 AUGUST 1943

On 21 August 1943, 252 Squadron made yet another visit to Preveza. This time just two aircraft were involved being those flown by Sergeant J. Evans and Flight Sergeant F. Hawthorne, JL595, and Flight Sergeant George Hobdell with Sergeant W. Lazenby, V8347.

Airborne from Berka III at 15.15 hours, the two Beaufighters attacked a 400-ton ship with canon and bombs, and, as can be seen in photographs (77), (78), and (79), scored near misses. German records state that two ships were damaged and that the defences were ineffective.

SUNDAY, 22 AUGUST 1943

The waters around Preveza were again the destination on 22 August 1943, with three aircraft being despatched. Only one, however, returned.

Led by Flight Lieutenant Keith Faulkner and Sergeant Geoff Goodes in EL281, the trio's initial target was a 2,000-ton tanker which was strafed and bombed without a positive result. The next vessel to be attacked, a 6-700 ton collier, was hit with strikes being observed. Flight Sergeant Norman Cresswell and Sergeant Frank Wright, in EL473/J, and Sergeant Donald Pearson and Sergeant Douglas Sherburn, in JL523/F, were last seen attacking the tanker; both aircraft failed to return having been shot down by Italian anti-aircraft fire. Cresswell and Wright were captured, whilst Pearson and Sherburn were killed.

Photographs (80), (81) and (82) show Faulkner's attack on the collier, SS *Bertha*. Built in 1922 by Smit, Rotterdam, as the Dutch cargo steamer SS *Trent*, in 1934 she became a French-registered vessel, the SS *Bacchus*. In 1943 she was taken over by the Germans and initially renamed *Brunhild*, this changing once again to *Bertha* in 1944. *Bertha* was sunk by an Allied submarine on 3 October 1943, at a position about forty miles north of Skiathos, Northern Sporades.

Images (83), (84) and (85), meanwhile, show other vessels being attacked. The first two possibly involve the tanker, whilst (85) appears to be a tug.

Faulkner and Goodes made their solitary landing back at Berka III at 16.20 hours.

MONDAY, 23 AUGUST 1943

On 23 August 1943, two Beaufighters of 603 Squadron, one crewed by Pilot Officer J.C. Dalziel and Sergeant J.H. Davies in EL478/F, the other by Flight Lieutenant John Crompton and Sergeant Henry Griffiths in JL625/R, took off from Berka III at 14.00 hours on an offensive sweep around Zante.

At 16.20 hours, they arrived over the town and attacked a ship of 500 tons which was moored in the harbour. The bombs failed to hit, though strikes by gunfire were recorded. However, as Crompton flew over the vessel, he was seen to make a steep bank to starboard, presumably as he had been hit by Flak. His wingtip struck the sea and the aircraft plunged into the water; both men on board were killed. Pictures (86) and (87) record both the attack and the demise of the Beaufighter. Though Dalziel's Beaufighter was also hit by Flak, he took evasive action and headed out to sea, landing safely at Berka at 18.40 hours.

THURSDAY, 2 SEPTEMBER 1943

On 2 September 1943, four aircraft of 252 Squadron – Wing Commander Dennis Butler and Flight Lieutenant Frank Quinn in JM250, Flight Sergeants Harry Humphries and Tom Burrows in JL595, Flight Sergeants George Hobdell and W.B. Lazenby in EL527 and recently-promoted and decorated Squadron Leader Keith Faulkner DFC and Flight Sergeant Geoff Goodes DFM in EL403 – took off from Berka III at 07.50 hours on an offensive sweep and recce of the west coast of Greece.

At a location given as 38.55N 20.53E, the formation spotted thirty parked vehicles. These were promptly attacked with cannon and machine-guns – as seen in pictures (88) and (89). After an explosion, and a number of the vehicles left burning, smoke and dust could be seen rising to 200 feet.

Shortly after, and north-west of Vonitsa, the Beaufighters spotted a 1,500-ton freighter, (90), which two aircraft immediately strafed; smoke was observed rising from the bridge. This was the 2,897 BRT Italian steamer *Palermo* (formerly the Greek *Athinai*) which reported being attacked off Preveza at 10.25 hours by four enemy aircraft – the attack also being pictured in (91), (92) and (93). A third Beaufighter then dropped two bombs, one of which exploded in the water six yards from the ship, whilst the last aircraft dropped another two bombs. These exploded to *Palermo*'s rear, after which the pilot strafed the luckless vessel. *Palermo* reported being damaged.

FRIDAY, 3 SEPTEMBER 1943

The day after 252 Squadron's attack on *Palermo*, a reconnaissance mission by a Baltimore of 203 Squadron encountered the damaged freighter at Vonitsa – picture (94). Unfortunately, 203 Squadron's Operations Record Book is incomplete and makes no mention of the crew.

MONDAY, 13 SEPTEMBER 1943

There was a rare combat success for 252 Squadron on 13 September 1943. At 13.03 hours, Flight Sergeant Desmond De Villiers and Flight Sergeant W.P. Fryer took off from Limassol, Cyprus, in V8347 to give fighter cover two four ships, one of which was the sloop *Gander*. Nine minutes later Flight Sergeant Alexander McKeown and Sergeant R. Dixon also took off in JL621 and met up with the other Beaufighter shortly afterwards.

Strangely the record of events in the Operations Record Book make no mention of what happened next but at 35.09N 31.39E, they spotted a Junkers Ju 88, the latter flying at an altitude of 300 feet and on a course of 130 degrees. This was a weather reconnaissance Ju 88 A-4 of *Wekusta* 26, *Werk Nummer* 140437 and coded 5M+Y, flown by *Feldwebel* Fritz Wolters.

De Villiers attacked three times from the starboard stern quarter from a range of 400 to 600 yards, but his cannon jammed and only his machine-guns fired. However, he did notice a small piece break away from the Ju 88's port engine. Alex McKeown then joined in the engagement, making eight attacks from the same range from both the port and starboard stern quarters.

The German pilot took violent evasive action, weaving and side-slipping as well as trying to corkscrew – (95) and (96). McKeown anticipated the final starboard turn, and set the Ju 88's starboard engine on fire, after which the German aircraft made a perfect landing on the sea eighty miles west of Cyprus at 13.00 hours. Two members of the Luftwaffe crew, and what was described as a rectangular box, were spotted in the water. In fact, all four men on board, Wolters, Unteroffizier Heinrich Schulze, Unteroffizier Hans Rader and meteorologist Dr Christian Theusner, were subsequently picked up by a high-speed launch and landed at Limassol.

FRIDAY, 17 SEPTEMBER 1943

Another successful and busy day for 252 Squadron was experienced on 17 September 1943. Four aircraft took off from Limassol at 12.35 hours on a shipping strike in the Dodecanese together, a mission undertaken with four aircraft from 227 Squadron. The 252 Squadron aircraft were those flown by Squadron Leader Keith Faulkner and Flight Sergeant Geoff Goodes (JM250), Flight Lieutenant Charles Delcour and Flight Sergeant Tom Lumsden (V8335), Flight Sergeant Harry Humphries and Flight Sergeant Tom Burrows (EL398) and Flight Sergeant Alex McKeown and Flight Sergeant R. Dixon (JM240).

Off Naxos, the formation spotted a small three-ship convoy, one vessel ahead on its own and the other two behind in line abreast. The larger ship was reported as being 'a three-island type of 5,000 tons', one of the others as 'a small coaster of 1,500 tons'. Also in attendance were two Arado Ar 196 floatplanes. The ships were the UJ-2104 *Darvik*, the 3,754-ton *Paula* and the 1,156-ton *Pluto*, carrying troops from Piraeus to Rhodes.

Faulkner climbed to attack the German aircraft, making a head-on attack. He saw cannon strikes along the fuselage of one of the floatplanes which then dived away sharply and landed alongside UJ-2104, one crew member being seen to get out. This Arado Ar 196 A-3, with the *Werk Nummer* 0185 and coded D1+EH of 1 *Staffel/Seeauklärungsgruppe* 126, later sank whilst under tow. Reported to have been shot down six kilometres north of the island of Los Angaeis, it had been crewed by Unteroffizier Fritz Schaar and Unteroffizier Herbert Schneider.

On the approach of the Beaufighters UJ-2104 turned through ninety degrees in an effort to bring all its guns to bear. Faulkner strafed both this ship and the coaster from bow to stern, noting cannon strikes on each. However, his aircraft was then hit by Flak which took out the starboard engine. JM250's bombs were jettisoned and Goodes then threw out the remainder of the ammunition, the defensive rear facing gun and the camera – but not before he had taken out the exposed film.

Belgian Charles Delcour then attacked the larger vessel, during which he observed near misses. His aircraft was, however, badly hit by Flak and the navigator, Tom Lumsden, killed. Humphries then strafed the lead ship scoring hits, after which he dropped two bombs on the larger vessel, one of which exploded close to the stern. Finally McKeown fired on the larger ship and scored two near misses with his bombs.

When the formation left the area, it was noted that the convoy had stopped and that grey smoke was rising to 100 feet from *Paula*. McKeown escorted Delcour back to Cyprus where the latter crash-landed at Limassol; all four 252 Squadron Beaufighters had landed by 18.40 hours. The small series of images numbered (97) through to, and including, (101) were taken during this mission.

The following day, the convoy was intercepted by HMS *Faulknor*, HMS *Eclipse* and the Greek destroyer *Vasilia Olga* off the island of Stampalia. The two merchant ships were sunk and UJ-2104 beached. Amongst the German casualties were the two rescued Arado 196 crew members, both of whom were duly reported missing.

97

100

101

MONDAY, 20 SEPTEMBER 1943

Early in the afternoon of 20 September 1943, two Beaufighters of 252 Squadron, being those crewed by Flight Sergeant Harry Humphries and Flight Sergeant Tom Burrows in JL999 and Flying Officer S.J.L. Smith and Pilot Officer Langford in EL501, together with four Beaufighters from 227 Squadron, spotted two E-Boats moored side-by-side in Vronti Bay on the island of Scarpanto together with a 350 to 400-ton coaster lying off shore and two barges.

Three bombs were dropped on the coaster by the 252 Squadron aircraft (a fourth bomb on EL501 hung up) missing by twenty to fifty yards – (102). JL999 then strafed the vessel, scoring hits. However, both aircraft were then forced to head for home due to the intense Flak coming from the E-boats (one of which may just be visible in the top left corner of the photograph). One Beaufighter of 227 Squadron was shot down by Flak with Flight Sergeant Wilf Webster and Flight Sergeant Edward Taylor being killed.

102

SATURDAY, 25 SEPTEMBER 1943

At 07.25 hours on 25 September 1943, four Beaufighters from 252 Squadron took off from their new base at Lakatamia in Cyprus to attack a torpedo boat reported aground at Prasonisi. The aircraft were those crewed by Squadron Leader Keith Faulkner and Flight Sergeant Geoff Goodes (EL403), Flight Sergeant Paddy Ward and Flight Sergeant P. Bernard (X8158), Flight Sergeant Lewis Passow and Flight Sergeant A. Underwood (EL501) and Flight Sergeant Des De Villiers and Flight Sergeant W.P. Fryer (JL899).

On reaching the target area, they spotted a 'Partenope-type torpedo boat in shallow water with its bows pointed west'. All aircraft strafed the enemy vessel and dropped a total of seven bombs (one of Lewis Passow's bombs hung up) of which one was thought to have hit the stern but did not explode. Three bombs were reported as near misses and three overshot, the attack being captured in pictures (103), (104) and (105).

When the Beaufighters departed the area black smoke was seen issuing from the boat – (106). This could still be seen from a distance of five miles. Defensive fire was weak and stopped when the boat was strafed. All aircraft had landed safely by 11.15 hours.

103

104

105

SUNDAY, 26 SEPTEMBER 1943

On 26 September 1943, three Beaufighters from 252 Squadron, as well as one from 227 Squadron, attacked the 1,870-ton German former seaplane tender and helicopter carrier, and now mine-layer, *Drache* (the former Yugoslav *Zmaj*) in Syros Harbour. Strangely, 252 Squadron's Operations Record Book only mentions that the crews involved were Flight Sergeants Lewis Passow and A. Underwood, in EL406, Flight Sergeant G. Thomas and Sergeant B.R. Richards, in JL899, and Flight Sergeant Paddy Ward and Flight Sergeant P. Bernard, in JM240.

German records confirm that the harbour and radio station were attacked with little damage caused. *Drache* was damaged by gunfire and the bombs dropped missed – (107) and (108). *Drache* would eventually be sunk by 252 and 603 squadrons in Port Vathi, Samos, on 22 September 1944.

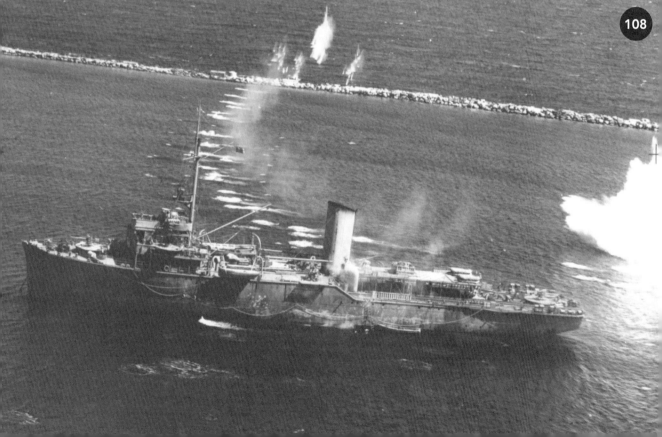

SATURDAY, 2 OCTOBER 1943

On 2 October 1943, a German convoy was spotted at sea heading east, initially off Paros and then Naxos. It consisted of five armed merchantmen, including the 4,470-ton *Sinfra* and the 2,500-ton liner *Citta di Savona*, as well as six F-boats and the 1,870-ton seaplane tender *Drache* (formerly the Yugoslav *Zmaj*). The following day, the convoy, by now with an enhanced escort, arrived off the island of Kos and at first light began landing troops, guns and vehicles, the operation codename being *Eisbär*.

At the same time, German bombers were overhead and put the airfield out of action, which, in turn, allowed German parachutists to land. It was initially decided that the Beaufighters of 46, 227 and 252 squadrons at Lakatamia would be used to help the British troops defending the island. The first mission was flown by 46 Squadron followed by 227 Squadron.

Seven aircraft of 252 Squadron duly took off at 06.10 hours. These were the Beaufighters flown by Wing Commander Dennis Butler and Flight Lieutenant Frank Quinn (JM230), Flight Sergeant Alex McKeown and Sergeant Frank Dixon (EL403), Flight Sergeant Lewis Passow and Flight Sergeant A. Underwood in (JL723), Flight Sergeant Harry Humphries and Flight Sergeant Tom Burrows (EL399), Flight Sergeant George Hobdell and Flight Sergeant W.B. Lazenby (JL899), Flight Sergeant G. Thomas and Sergeant B.R. Richards (JM240) and, finally, Pilot Officer John Barrett and Pilot Officer A.S. Haddon (V8347).

At 08.30 hours, the Beaufighter crews spotted a 3,000-ton ship with a small escort two miles off the coast. A stationary E-boat (probably UJ-2102 *Brigitta*) was also seen two miles south-south-east of these ships. Whilst Flight Sergeant Thomas attacked the escort with gunfire and one bomb (the other hung up), the remainder attacked the other two ships also with bombs and gunfire (albeit one aircraft had both bombs hung up). The crews reported no definite results on the escorts, though two columns of smoke were seen rising from the other ships. Flak was intense, with Harry Humphries, Tom Burrows and John Barrett all being slightly wounded. All aircraft landed at 10.45 hours.

Other sorties that day were flown by 46, 89 and 227 squadrons – one of which resulted in the death of Wing Commander George Reid, Commanding Officer of 46 Squadron, who was shot down by an Arado 196.

For its part, 252 Squadron took off again for Kos at 12.55 hours with the three aircraft involved being led by Squadron Leader Horace Hubbard and Pilot Officer G.E. Jones in EL528. Arriving off the island, they identified a concentration of enemy shipping at anchor, all of which put up an intense Flak barrage. Above, they spotted Arado 196 floatplanes and chased one which headed towards the ships and the safety of the German Flak. All three aircraft landed safely at 17.35 hours.

Photographs (109) through to, and including, (113) all come from the first sortie that day. German records state: 'Several landing groups were assembled in the Naxos area on 2 October 1943. On 3 October 1943, between 0400 and 0430 hours, the first wave was landed by surprise at three points of the Island of Kos with naval landing craft. Two landings were made on the south coast by 0700. These were attacked by enemy planes, of which two were shot down.

'The four steamers of the northern group were unloaded to some extent under mortar fire and shelling. This group also was attacked by 'planes, of which three were shot down. The steamer *Citta di Savona* and submarine chaser UJ-2102 were bombed and machine-gunned by seven low flying enemy 'planes; only minor casualties were caused and one enemy 'plane was shot down.'

FRIDAY, 22 OCTOBER 1943

On 22 October 1943, during operations in the Dodecanese with the British destroyer HMS *Hurworth*, the Greek destroyer *Adrias* struck a mine which tore off her bow near the island of Kalymnos.

The Flotilla Commander, onboard *Hurworth*, ordered Commander Toumbas to abandon ship but while trying to come to *Adrias'* rescue, *Hurworth* also hit a mine and sank taking 143 men with her. In spite of the damage suffered, *Adrias* now took on the survivors of *Hurworth* (her captain amongst them) and managed to reach the nearby coast at Gümüslük in Turkey with twenty-one of her crew dead and thirty wounded. After some minor repairs and despite missing her bow, the ship sailed on 1 December 1943, and after a trip of 730 nautical miles managed to reach Alexandria on 6 December 1943.

On 24 October 1943, 252 Squadron flew eleven sorties as cover for three ships rescuing personnel from *Adria*. Picture (114) was taken by Wing Commander Dennis Butler in JL723, who was flying with his usual navigator Flight Lieutenant Frank Quinn. Butler was leading three other aircraft which took off at 11.54 hours and landed without incident at 16.54 hours.

SUNDAY, 14 NOVEMBER 1943

At 11.35 hours on 14 November 1943, four Beaufighters from 46 Squadron – being those flown by Flight Lieutenant David Crerar and Pilot Officer L. Charles (JL913), Flying Officer B.F. Wild and Flight Sergeant R.W. Gibbon (JL898), Flying Officer Joe Horsfall and Flight Sergeant Jim Colley (JM248) and Warrant Officer Ron Lindsey and Flight Sergeant Alfred Gardner (JL894) – lifted off from Laketamia together with four aircraft from 227 Squadron. The crews had been ordered to carry out a strike against the island of Leros.

When the Beaufighters were ten miles east of the island they spotted a Heinkel He 111 some four miles away flying at fifty feet. This was a He 111 H-11 of *Einsatzstaffel/Kampfgeschwader* 100, *Werk Nummer* 8011 and coded 6N+EP, flown by Unteroffizier Walter Pink.

Crerar gave chase, closed to 100 yards and opened fire, scoring hits, after which Flying Officer Wild fired a five-second burst – three seconds later the He 111 ditched. Pink, his observer, Feldwebel Kurt Bruder, and radio operator, Feldwebel Johann Sunnenschein, were rescued, though suffering varying degrees of injury. Gefreiter Helmut Grundke, the flight engineer, was killed. Picture (115) shows the Heinkel under attack.

Bombing attacks were in progress on the island after which the Beaufighters were instructed to return to base. It was then that six Messerschmitt Bf 109s were spotted approaching from Leros. The Beaufighters dropped their bombs and tried to escape. However, JL894, being flown by Ron Lindsey, was attacked by former Battle of Britain fighter pilot Hauptmann Ernst Düllberg of *Stab* III/ *Jagdgeschwader* 27. The Beaufighter made a vertical climb, half rolled and, at 13.35 hours, dived steeply into the sea exploding on impact. This was Düllberg's twenty-second kill of the war. All that was subsequently seen of the Beaufighter and its crew were fuel tanks floating on the water.

The remaining Beaufighters scattered and headed for Turkey, but the German fighters gave chase. Joe Horsfall was not seen and when called up on the radio nothing was heard; he had already been shot down by Oberfähnrich Alexander Ottnad of 8 *Staffel/Jagdgeschwader* 27 at 13.36 hours. It was Ottnad's third kill of the war. The surviving 46 Squadron aircraft landed at 17.00 hours.

THURSDAY, 16 DECEMBER 1943

At 07.55 hours on 16 December 1943, Baltimore FW617 of 454 Squadron got airborne from Berka on what was described as an 'Adriatic Recce'. The Baltimore was flown by an Australian crew, namely Squadron Leader M. Moore (Pilot), Flight Sergeant C. Lingham (Navigator), Flying Officer D. George and Pilot Officer T. Strickland (both Wireless Operator/Air Gunners).

Moore landed back at base without incident at 13.55 hours. The somewhat bland entry in the Operations Record Book just mentions that the crew had observed something – which is clearly shown in photograph (116) but unfortunately the location was not recorded.

Part III
1944

SUNDAY, 23 JANUARY 1944

At 07.55 hours on 23 January 1944, four Beaufighters of 227 (Long Range Fighter) Squadron lifted off from Berka III for an offensive sweep off south-west Greece. Leading the small force was Commanding Officer Wing Commander John Buchanan, with Warrant Officer Reg Howes as his navigator, in JL910/S. The other three aircraft were JL905/Q (Flying Officer Richard Hutchison/Flight Sergeant Les Sawle), EL270/N (Flying Officer Ken Judd/Sergeant Allan Thomas) and ER228/F (Flight Sergeant J.R. Cramp/Sergeant L.A. Everett).

At 10.16 hours they attacked the harbour at Koroni having spotted two caiques of 80 and 150 tons and what was described as a motor launch – the attack being seen in pictures (1) and (2). All aircraft strafed the ships, after which Buchanan dropped a single bomb which blew up the motor launch's stern. Many hits were seen on the caiques. At this point Hutchison radioed, 'Trouble, starboard engine, going back'. Both he and his navigator were later reported killed.

Four minutes later the remaining three Beaufighters attacked Kalamata, (3), having identified five caiques there under construction, a 120 ton caique loaded with barrels, eight smaller caiques and a white-painted 200-ton schooner alongside the quay. The Beaufighters concentrated on the schooner with two bombs being dropped, both of which just missed – images (4) through to (9) detail the attack on this vessel, the last providing a graphic illustration of just how low the Beaufighters were. Each aircraft attacked four times and the schooner was seen well ablaze as they left.

Flak had been weak at first but increased with each Beaufighter's pass. Ken Judd reported he had been hit in the tail, the other two crews noting a large hole in both sides at the end of the fuselage. The three aircraft then turned for home. Though they encountered enemy shipping en route, the decision was made not to attack.

On entering the circuit to land at Berka III, Judd reported that his starboard engine was giving trouble. Shortly afterwards, at 13.00 hours, EL270 crashed five miles south of the airfield. Judd was killed, whilst Thomas survived, albeit injured.

WEDNESDAY, 26 JANUARY 1944

On 26 January 1944, Wing Commander John Buchanan and Warrant Officer Reg Howes, once again in JL910/S, led another three aircraft of 227 Squadron on an offensive sweep south of Morea. The other crews were Flying Officer Alexander Will and Flying Officer Brian Findley in JL708/E, Flight Lieutenant John Bliss and Flying Officer Norman Rigby in EL467/J and Sergeant Sidney Appleton and Sergeant Jack Fenton in EL509/K.

Taking off from Berka III at 08.48 hours, the four crews first noted a wrecked ship and two caiques in Kapsali Bay at 10.51 hours, as well as spotting a radio station to the west of the Bay. At 10.35 hours, they flew over a caique flying a red cross in St Nikolo Bay and, five minutes later, spotted another radio mast at Cape Spathi. So far, no attacks had been carried out – but that was about to change.

At 10.47 hours a small caique was seen in Xili Bay and, immediately after, a much larger caique tied alongside the jetty at Gythion. All aircraft carried out two strafing attacks; images (10), (11) and (12) were taken at this point in the flight (note the Beaufighter banking to the left over the promentary in the first two pictures). Yet again Buchanan scored a direct hit with a bomb which resulted in the caique exploding. The victim was *Agios Spyridon* which was reported sunk in an air attack at Gythion. By this stage, the enemy anti-aircraft gunners had woken up and Appleton reported his aircraft had been hit near the port engine, though he elected to continue with the mission.

At 11.17 hours, a two-masted 80 ton caique was spotted anchored in a bay and the aircraft duly attacked, all of them dropping bombs. However, Will's Beaufighter was seen to crash into the sea having failed to pull out of a dive. The aircraft disintegrated – no survivors being seen (both Will and Findley were killed).

The remaining three aircraft continued on to Kalamata and, in a repeat of the sortie three days earlier, attacked a number of caiques under construction, hitting four, before the anti-aircraft defences opened up. The latter again hit Appleton's Beaufighter, this time in the starboard wing root.

On their way out, the raiders attacked a moored caique and then, over Koroni, strafed more caiques under construction. It was noted that the one which had been attacked on 23 January 1944 had indeed had its stern blown off. In picture (13) a part of Koroni Castle, which is located on a headland at the eastern end of Koroni bay, can be seen, whilst (14) is of the quayside at Koroni. The shot in (15), meanwhile, was taken at another location during the mission – once again note the low-flying Beaufighters.

The three Beaufighters landed without further incident at 13.47 hours.

TUESDAY, 8 FEBRUARY 1944

On 8 February 1944, 227 Squadron was tasked with another offensive sweep of the eastern Aegean, the sortie being led by Wing Commander John Buchanan and Warrant Officer Reg Howes, this time in JL731/Q. Taking off at 0855 hours, the other three Beaufighters were EL228/P (Flying Officer Bill Davies and Flight Sergeant Geoff Brown), JL911/E (Flying Officer L.R. Walker and Flight Sergeant R.J. Roll) and JL595 (Flight Sergeants Len Hibbert and Harry Parker).

At 10.55 hours, whilst flying at just fifty feet, the four Beaufighters spotted three caiques of about 60-80 tons and another of 100 tons moored in a channel off Poros – as seen in (16). There were also quite a number of smaller craft against the town quay, as well as a 100-ton barge. Noting a German flag flying from a quayside building, each aircraft made three attacks with bombs, machine-guns and cannon. One of the Beaufighters can be seen making its attack in (17), (18) and (19). Though all of the bombs failed to strike anything, the four caiques were well hit by cannon fire, so much so that one sank and the remainder were badly damaged. Indeed, the larger vessel could be seen smouldering as the attackers departed.

Two of the aircraft then attacked another caique which, laden with sacks, was heading north from Poros. After the second Beaufighter's pass, it could be seen to be settling in the water.

The four Beaufighters then headed out over Sparti and coast-crawled to Cape Matapan. Apart from a short burst of fire against a forty-ton ship, there was little else to report and they all landed safely at Berka III at 13.40 hours. The bridge in picture (20) was photographed during the flight.

WEDNESDAY, 9 FEBRUARY 1944

On 9 February 1944, see six aircraft from 227 Squadron, yet again led by Wing Commander John Buchanan and Warrant Officer Reg Howes in JL731/Q, carried out an offensive sweep of Katakolio, Navarin and Kalamata. The other crews were Flying Officers John Corlett and Gwyn Williams in EL228/P, Squadron Leader Dennis Bennett and Flight Sergeant T.R. Bignold in JL911/E, Flying Officer J.W. Edwards and Flight Sergeant H.N. Allen in EL467/J, Flight Sergeant Sidney Appleton and Sergeant Jack Fenton in JL595/A and, finally, Flight Lieutenant James Holland and Flight Sergeant J. Templeton in JM237/M.

Taking off at 07.00 hours, they reached Kalamata at 08.59 hours, but saw nothing of interest. Continuing, the crews spotted a radar station near Methoni, before heading on to Kiparissa, where they noted a sunken ship in the harbour and a long line of people outside a shop.

So far, little had happened, even though they had been subjected to light, sporadic and ineffective Flak. At 09.34 hours, they spotted a 300-ton auxiliary two-masted schooner in Katakalon harbour, after which they flew on Killini.

Seeing nothing there, they decided to return to Katakalon and at 09.50 hours, all six aircraft attacked the schooner they had spotted earlier – captured in pictures (21) through to (25). Each aircraft carried out between five and six attacks; eight bombs fell within a few yards of the hapless ship. Hit countless times by gunfire, it was left riddled with gaping holes and a mast shot away. The schooner was smoking as the Beaufighters headed for Navarin and home, landing at 12.30 hours.

FRIDAY, 11 FEBRUARY 1944

Only three of 227 Squadron's aircraft would participate in the offensive sweep scheduled for 11 February 1944. Taking off from Berka III at 09.55 hours, the trio comprised JL897/W (Wing Commander John Buchanan and Warrant Officer Reg Howes), EL467/J (Flight Sergeants E.C. James and Allan Thomas) and JL585/A (Warrant Officer Keith Wright and Flight Sergeant Gordon Jones).

At midday, the three Beaufighters sighted an eighty-ton caique and a 200-ton motor-driven barge which were anchored 200 yards apart in the harbour at Spetsai. All aircraft made two attacks, with Flight Sergeant James scoring a direct hit on the barge with his second attack. Debris and a pall of smoke rose from the vessel, which was observed to be settling in the water as the aircraft left. The barge can be seen under fire in pictures (26) to (29).

The attack, though, had not been trouble-free, as the port engine of Keith Wright's Beaufighter was seen to catch fire. He was forced to ditch to the east of the harbour; the aircraft sank immediately; there was no sign of a dinghy. It later transpired that Wright had been killed but his navigator was reported safe and well.

The remaining two aircraft then headed for Ieraka and attacked two 100-ton caiques only for the cannon doors on John Buchanan's aircraft to be blown off. Both crews reported extreme turbulence in the target area so they elected not to attack a second time, landing back at Berka III at 15.10 hours.

This was the last successful mission for the highly experienced Wing Commander John Buchanan DSO, DFC, who is recognised as the top-scoring Beaufighter strike pilot of the war, being credited with three enemy aircraft destroyed, another six damaged, one shared damaged, and another destroyed having been strafed on the water. On 16 February 1944, Buchanan was shot down whilst attacking shipping at Nauplia, sixty miles south-west of Athens. His Beaufighter, EL467/J, was hit by Flak in the starboard engine and he ditched successfully. Both crew were seen in the water, Buchanan clinging to a fuel or oil tank. Both men managed to get into a dinghy, but although Reg Howes was later reported safe, John Buchanan died of exposure and dehydration.

SUNDAY, 27 FEBRUARY 1944

At 09.20 hours on 27 February 1944 four 227 Squadron aircraft took off from Berka III on yet another offensive sweep. They were the Beaufighters crewed by Flight Lieutenant John Bliss and Flying Officer Norman Rigby (EL467/J), Flight Sergeants G.S. Bolton and H.J. Collins (EL931), Flying Officer Bill Davies and Flight Sergeant Geoff Brown (EL509/K), and Flight Sergeant Len Hibbert and Sergeant Harry Parker (T5170/C).

At 11.37 hours, they attacked Flak positions at Messolongi only for Bill Davies' aircraft to be hit in the starboard engine, this catching fire. Davies' ditched, but both crewmen were killed. The three remaining aircraft then attacked a tug headed for Messolonghi and left it severely damaged – picture (30). The trio then returned to Berka III, landing at 14.55 hours.

WEDNESDAY, 31 MAY 1944

During the evening of 31 May 1944, a substantial convoy set sail from Piraeus on mainland Greece bound for Candia (Heraklion Harbour) in Crete. It consisted of the merchant ships *Tanais*, *Gertrud* and *Sabine* escorted by four of what the Germans called Torpedoboot Ausland or T-Boots, (TA-14, TA-16, TA-17 and TA-19), three submarine hunters or UJ-Boot (UJ-2101, UJ-2105 and UJ-2110) and two smaller fast torpedo boats (R34 and R211). The convoy was not only protected by barrage balloons but a number of Messerschmitt Bf 109s from either 13 *Staffel/Jagdgeschwader* 27 (13./JG 27) or 5./*JG* 51, four Junkers Ju 88s from possibly 3 *Staffel/ Aufklärungsgruppe* 33, and four Arado Ar 196 floatplanes from 4 *Staffel/Seeaufklärungsgruppe* 126 (4/126).

The importance of this convoy was not lost on the Allies, as Air Marshal Keith Park, Air Officer Commanding Middle East Command, indicated in a cable to the Station Commander at Gambut: 'As the Navy have no ships available, it remains to the Air Force to put this convoy down. The German military garrison in Crete is badly in need of supplies and the destruction of one or more ships of this convoy will be an important victory. There is bound to be Flak and there may be fighter opposition and the AOC-in-C wishes you good luck and good hunting in your important mission.'

Allied aircraft shadowed the convoy throughout 1 June 1944, losing a Baltimore of 454 Squadron RAAF, that flown by Warrant Officer George Liels, early in the afternoon. Picture (31) is a shot of the convoy whilst being shadowed by a 454 Squadron Baltimore.

Early that evening, as the convoy was just forty miles out from Crete, the order to attack was given. A total of sixty-three aircraft were involved, attacking in two waves. The first wave consisted of twelve Marauders of 24 Squadron SAAF, fifteen Baltimores of 15 Squadron SAAF, and three Baltimores of 454 Squadron, all of which were escorted by seven Spitfires from 94 Squadron and six Spitfires and four Mustangs of 213 Squadron. The second wave was made up from Beaufighters from 252 Squadron (ten in number), 603 Squadron (eight), 227 Squadron (two) and 16 Squadron SAAF (four). The Beaufighters had two roles – Flak suppression and, for the majority, attacking with rockets.

The Operations Record Book for 252 Squadron explains the build up to the attack: 'During the early hours of the morning of the 1st of June, orders were received for eight Beaufighters to proceeded to Gambut for a strike against a convoy sighted by a Wellington of 38 Squadron … It was known that the forces in Crete were extremely short of supplies and it was anticipated that the enemy would endeavour to run a convoy to relieve the garrison there. It was decided to send all our serviceable aircraft and crews to Gambut and accordingly 10 Beaufighters with 13 crews departed from Mersa Matruh for Gambut at first light … Eight aircraft as the striking force and two as anti-Flak.'

At 18.57 hours, the convoy was sighted by the leading Allied bomber twenty-seven miles north of Candia. At 19.03 hours, the Marauders, followed two minutes later by the Baltimores, attacked. Much of the bombing was inaccurate although a hit was claimed on *Sabine* which was leading the convoy. Turning for home unscathed, the bombers now passed the Beaufighters streaking in for the attack at low level. Their attack would be far more dramatic and effective – although it appeared, initially at least, that things might not go as planned.

The formation of twenty-six Beaufighters took off from Gambut at 16.28 hours led by Wing Commander Bryce 'Willie' Meharg, the Commanding Officer of 252 Squadron. At 19.08 hours, the formation, less two aircraft which had to return early with mechanical trouble, approached the convoy from the west, by which time it was twenty-five miles north of Candia. Willie Meharg immediately gave the order to attack. Picture (32) was taken when the convoy came under attack by 252 Squadron. Image (33) depicts one of the barrage balloons flying over the enemy ships.

The German ships put up a formidable wall of Flak; before he could do anything, Meharg's Beaufighter was hit and, with its port wing on fire, dived into the sea on the east side of the convoy.

Whilst picture (34) was taken as the warships were attacked by 603 Squadron, to the right is believed to be crash of Meharg's Beaufighter. Image (35) was also taken during 603 Squadron's strike. It was thought by the other crews that Meharg and his navigator, Flying Officer Ernest Thompson, had been killed. As Thompson later wrote, the pair had in fact survived:

'I was wondering vaguely in my confused mind why everything was so still and peaceful and slowly I became conscious of the fact that my body was in water which was steadily coming up to my head. Suddenly I realised fully everything that had happened and knew that I must get out quickly before the aircraft sank.

'Two mistakes in the next few seconds might have cost me my life there and then. I tried to throw myself out of the hatch but I had not released the seat strap harness which held me so securely at the moment of the terrific impact with the water. Frantically the straps were undone and I dived through the hatch to be pulled up short with a sudden jolt which seemed almost to break my neck. The lead from my headphones to the intercom socket was still plugged in but fortunately the strain jerked the earphones from the helmet.

'As I came up to the surface my eye caught sight of the yellow rubber dinghy not more than 10 yards away. I struck out for it immediately, only to found that the enemy fire had accounted for this as well – it was holed and useless.

'However, this shattering blow was temporarily forgotten when I turned to look back towards what was left of the aircraft. There was the nose and the pilot's cockpit still above the water and I was so relieved to see this that I found myself shouting "Willie! Willie!" and trying to swim my fastest at the same time.

'I was about half-way there when I saw the Skipper already in the sea hanging on to a small piece of floating wood. I called out "You OK Willie?" and heard him reply "I'm all right. How about yourself?"

'Yes, I thought for the first time, how am I? I glanced down at my left arm and it looked horrible, a piece of raw flesh with streamers of skin trailing in the water like the white of an egg. But there was no pain at all-yet.

'We were both holding on to the plank when what was left of the aircraft went down, nearly taking us with it. Heaven knows how much oil came flooding to the surface, covering us with filth. No matter how much we kicked we could not make clear water and finally we gave up trying but still clung to the plank.'

The attack that followed the loss of Willie Meharg's crash was nothing short of devastating for the German convoy. The first two 252 Squadron aircraft to attack were the anti-Flak aircraft flown by Warrant Officer J.S. Bates and Pilot Officer H.A. Stevenson. They singled out one of the destroyers at the rear of the convoy, firing a total of fourteen rockets before opening fire with cannon. Squadron Leader Ian Butler then attacked *Sabine*, followed by Pilot Officer Arthur Pierce; between them they fired sixteen rockets which apparently blew off *Sabine*'s stern.

Flying Officer G.G. Tuffin fired on an unidentified escort, leaving it spewing huge clouds of smoke and steam. Both (36) and (37) were taken during his attack.

Warrant Officer F.C.H. Jones then hit a destroyer in the centre of the convoy before peeling off to attack *Tanais*. Pilot Officer J.A.T. Mackintosh and Warrant Officer S.E. Legat, for their part, attacked a destroyer and *Sabine* respectively, but missed. Finally, Pilot Officer Bill Davenport attacked *Gertrud* with eight 60lb rockets, scoring direct hits on the bridge and superstructure and recording seeing a huge sheet of flame and black smoke.

The remaining three Beaufighter squadrons also carried out similar attacks on the convoy. The Allied force left *Sabine* burnt out; so much so that she had to be torpedoed. Pictures (38) and (39) depicts *Sabine* under attack by 16 Squadron SAAF - note the vehicles and stores on the deck.

Gertrud was also well ablaze but it was possible for her to be towed into Candia Harbour. *Tanais* had been severely damaged but managed to make it to harbour later that evening. Two UJ-boats, UJ-2105 and UJ-2101, were sunk and TA-16 badly damaged.

The Allied aircraft involved in the attack did not get off scot free. For its part, 252 Squadron reported that four aircraft had returned with Flak damage. In addition to the loss of Wing Commander Meharg, Flight Sergeant Ron Atkinson and his navigator, Sergeant Dennis Parsons, of 603 Squadron were reported missing, whilst the Beaufighter of Flying Officer John Jones and his navigator Flying Officer Ron Wilson, of 227 Squadron, was so badly damaged by anti-aircraft fire that during their return they crash-landed on the north-east coast of Crete, both men being taken prisoner.

Finally, the Beaufighter of Captain E.A. Barrett and Lieutenant A.J. Haupt of 16 Squadron SAAF lost its port engine to Flak and crash-landed at Hierapetra in the south-east of Crete. Both Barrett and Haupt were captured. Picture (40) shows Barrett's and Haupt's stricken Beaufighter making for Crete.

German records indicate that the anti-aircraft defenders claimed six Beaufighters, four alone by the gunners on TA-16. Curiously, the Ar 196s of 4/126 claimed a total of four Beaufighters, one each by Oberfeldwebel Kurt Chalupka, Oberfähnrich Fritz Rupp, Oberfeldwebel Werner Kurth and Unteroffizier Hässler.

Although Flight Sergeant Fred Sheldrick of 227 Squadron claimed to have shot down an Arado and a 454 Squadron crew reported seeing a Bf 109 crash into the sea, the reality was that only three Arados returned damaged by friendly fire.

The 252 Squadron diarist also recorded the following: 'The day's operations was a great success and the weather very good, there being practically nil cloud and unlimited visibility. The sea was clam and the wind light.

'The news of the successes of our aircraft had an intoxicating effect amongst all members of the Squadron and congratulatory messages were received … It is hoped that the enemy will soon run more convoys to his garrison in Crete but in view of the catastrophe of his convoy of 1st June, it is thought extremely unlikely that he will do so.'

As the Beaufighters had returned home, two British aircrew were still waiting to be rescued. Flying Officer Thompson continued:

'Looking away from the convoy, we simultaneously sighted a small yellow object about 40 yards away and recognized it as the dinghy pack. What luck! Willie kicked off his shoes and swam towards it. He brought it back and together we opened it without a word, though each of us were thinking of that precious Very pistol and its three cartridges. It was our only hope.

'The gun was quickly assembled and now we settled down to wait for the circling aircraft to be in the most favourable position for observation. Three cartridges meant three chances. Willie held the pistol aloft and at what he thought was the right moment fired it into the air. A red star sped 100 feet skywards and then descended leaving a trail of smoke. We waited with our hearts beating but it was soon obvious that our God-sent effort to claim attention had gone by unobserved. The pistol was reloaded and again we waited.

'A few minutes later two Arado 196s mad a very wide orbit and were approaching close to us. This was it. Please God make them look this way.

'Again the little red distress star sailed through the air and this time our prayers were answered. Almost immediately they turned and came in our direction. One of them did a tight turn directly over our heads and I watched the gunner closely but his guns did not move. He was in a very good position to shoot at us but obviously he had no such intention. Maybe they'll land and pick us up-they have floats I thought.

'A few minutes later, the second aircraft flew directly over our heads, very low and dropped a smoke float. Smoke billowed forth and our position was obvious for all to see. Every one of the aircraft came over to have a look and the Mes and Jus stood on their wingtips above us. Their crews seemed to be enjoying themselves immensely.

'Then we saw the Arados land and taxi towards us. Willie hastily threw the gun away just in case and our saviours came alongside. Willie made for one machine and I went to the other where the gunner was standing on the starboard float. "Climb on the float" he ordered, surprising me with his very good English. But I found it impossible to obey. My leg seemed paralysed and my arm and had were so tender that I couldn't bear to touch anything. Somehow he managed to haul me out of the sea and into the aircraft and I took his seat at the rear, chilled to the bone. The air was now at my burns and it was incredibly painful.

'The engine of the other plane roared and I looked round to see it take off. We were turning into wind when the gunner told me to sit on the floor. I did so and he began to unwrap a first-aid dressing but the aircraft began to leap forward and after a number of bumps, it suddenly became smooth. Never was I so glad to be airborne.'

The following evening, a mixed force of Marauders and Baltimores attacked Candia Harbour, sinking *Gertrud* and TA-16, returning without loss.

There is a sad postscript to the events of 1 June 1944. Only one freighter had survived the attack. Although badly damaged, the 1,500 ton *Tanais* was declared seaworthy and on the night of 8 June 1944 set sail for Piraeus. A few days before, the Germans had decided to round up the majority of the Cretan Jewish community. Together with some 600 captured Resistance fighters and Italian PoWs, 265 Jews had been loaded on to *Tanais*. At 02.31 hours on 9 June 1944, she was spotted by the British submarine HMS *Vivid*, commanded by Lieutenant John Varley, thirty-three miles north-east of Piraeus. At 03.13 hours, Varley gave the order to fire four torpedoes, two of which hit *Tanais*. Fifteen minutes later, the freighter slipped beneath the Mediterranean taking with her countless victims, at least 100 of them children.

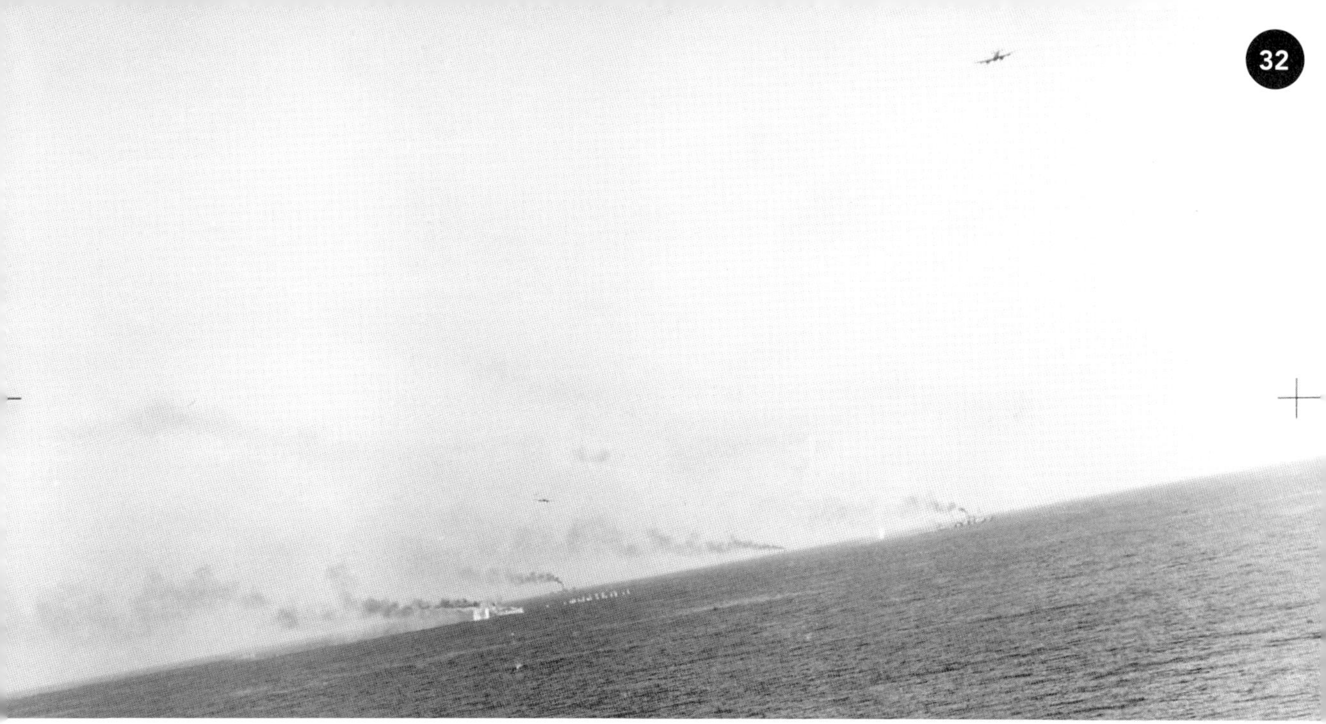

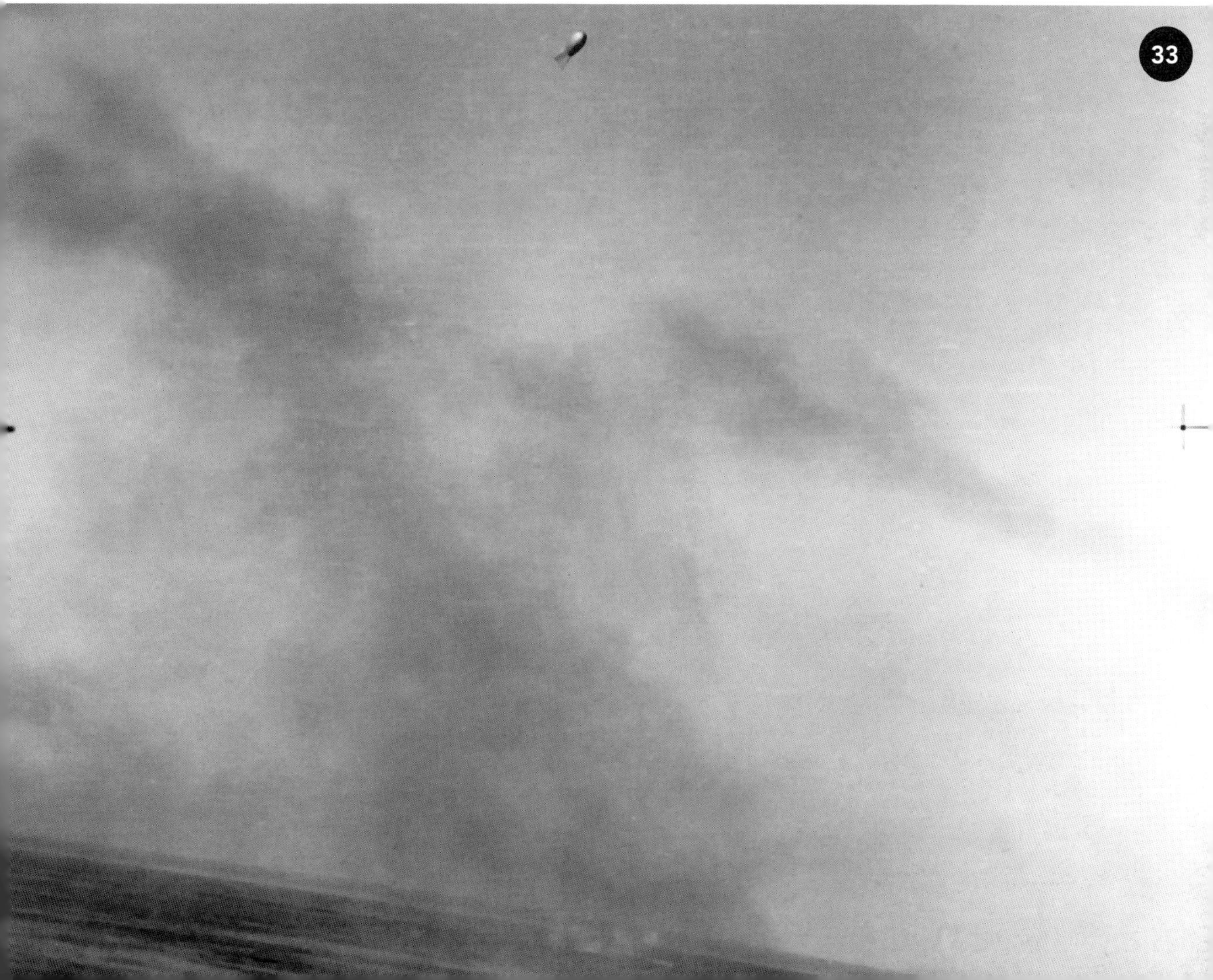

MONDAY, 19 JUNE 1944

On 19 June 1944, eight Bristol Beaufighters of 252 Squadron lifted off from Mersa Matruh in Egypt on an offensive sweep of the Aegean. The lead aircraft was flown by Flight Lieutenant Charles Whyatt, his navigator being Flight Sergeant R.A. Barrett.

Just before 16.00 hours, the formation, which was just south-west of the island of Kalymnos, came across what they described as 'a convoy consisted of one destroyer and two E-boats travelling at a speed of 15 knots on a course of 180 degrees … There was an air escort of two Arados, one flying at 500 feet and the other flying at sea level. The two E-boats were in line abreast behind the destroyer.'

The destroyer was in fact TA-19, formerly the Italian destroyer *Calatafimi*. *Calatafimi* was one of four Curtatone-class destroyers, these being the first Italian destroyers to be built after the end of the First World War. The 900-ton *Calatafimi* was launched in March 1923, being commissioned in May 1924. She was armed with four 102mm guns, two 76mm guns, six 31.2mm machine-guns and was capable of launching torpedoes and dropping mines. She had been quite a prize when captured, along with her sister ship *Castelfidardo*, by the Germans at Piraeus on 9 September 1943. *Castelfidardo* became TA16 – she would be badly mauled by Beaufighters on 1 June 1944, only to be sunk in a bombing raid at Heraklion the following day. However, despite her defences, on this day TA-19 would prove vulnerable to the rocket-armed Beaufighters.

The Beaufighters struck at 15.58 hours. Charles Whyatt was the first to attack, firing all of his eight 25lb rocket projectiles at TA-19; a flash was seen, along with flames coming from the rear of the warship.

Four more Beaufighters then launched themselves at TA-19. They later reported two underwater hits, two possible direct hits near the bridge and two direct hits aft. All five Beaufighters also raked the warship with cannon fire. The attack on TA-19 is illustrated by images (41) through to (44). In (44), note the rocket trails from the previous Beaufighter's attack, the aircraft is just visible banking to the left over the warship, and the rockets in the foreground.

Meanwhile, Australian pilot Warrant Officer J.S. Bates, together with his navigator Pilot Officer Frank Gresswell, was forced to tackle an Arado Ar 196 from *Seeaufklärungsgruppe* 126 as he was running in to attack TA-19. Flying at an altitude of 400 feet, Bates opened fire with cannon – picture (45). He did not observe any strikes but did see smoke coming from the floatplane's starboard wing. The Arado then banked off to starboard and orbited to the north of the convoy, which allowed Gresswell to get in an inconclusive burst of machine-gun fire before resuming the attack on the most easterly E-boat, spraying it with cannon and machine-gun fire. The Ar 196 of 3/126, an A-5 variant with the *Werk Nummer* 0365 and coded D1+CL, reported suffering minor damage from an RAF aircraft off the island of Caline.

As the engagement unfolded, Flying Officer Cyril Mason and his navigator, Flight Sergeant J.R. Smith, targeted another two Arados, whilst Flight Lieutenant Clement 'Chick' Fowler and his navigator, Flight Sergeant S. McAughtry, was forced, due to the close proximity of so many eager Beaufighters, to only attack TA-19 with cannon fire for fear of hitting one of his squadron with a rocket.

However, 252 Squadron did not get off unscathed. Aircraft NE546/Q, crewed by Pilot Officer Bill Davenport and Flight Sergeant Cecil Grainger, was seen with its starboard engine on fire, ditch immediately after. The Beaufighter floated long enough for the two crew to get into a dinghy – see (46) and (47). A small caique was seen just south of Kalymnos Harbour, five miles from the ditching. Any hope that it was friendly was dashed a few days later when the Germans reported both Davenport and Grainger had been picked up safe and sound. Put ashore on Leros, the pair were soon transferred to a prisoner of war camp, Davenport to Stalag Luft III and Grainger to Stalag Luft VII.

As 252 Squadron turned for home, TA-19, badly damaged, headed for the Greek mainland for repairs. Her future would, however, be short. At 17.05 hours on 9 August 1944, she was discovered off Karlovassi by the Greek submarine *Pipinos* (formerly HMS *Veldt*), commanded by Lieutenant Commander C. Loundras, and soon after torpedoed and sunk.

41

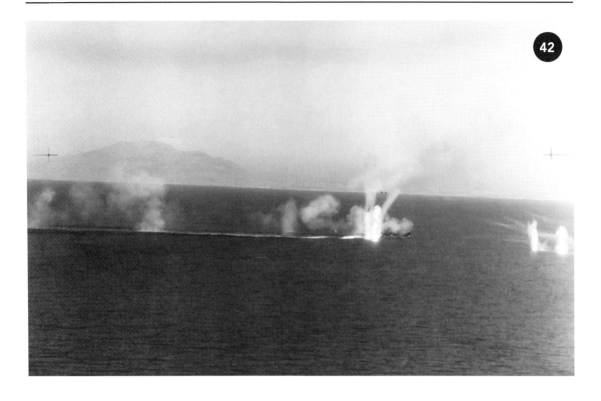

TUESDAY, 27 JUNE 1944

On 27 June 1944, 252 Squadron launched eight Beaufighters on an offensive sweep of Miabella Bay. Led by Flight Lieutenant Charles Whyatt and Flight Sergeant R.A. Barrett in NE704/X, the aircraft were airborne from Mersa Matruh between 07.42 and 07.55 hours.

The first shots were fired by Whyatt against a gun position at Spinalongha at 09.58 hours. Six minutes later, the formation was approaching Sitia Harbour where they spotted a possible coaster of 100 feet and an armed auxiliary caique. Again Charles Whyatt attacked first, followed by Warrant Officer S.E. Legat and Flight Sergeant R.A. Paskell in NE499/P, Flying Officer E.M.G Ferguson and Flight Sergeant L. Douglas in NE468/Y and then Flying Officer C.H. Mason and Flight Sergeant J.R. Smith in NE497/F.

All of the crews reported numerous hits on the coaster with cannon. Meanwhile, Warrant Officer F.C.H. Jones and Sergeant I.P. Cowl in NE479/E attacked the coaster with a long burst of cannon fire, followed by three rapid pairs of rockets, all of which overshot. Finally, Warrant Officer A.R. O'Neil and Sergeant G.W.A Long, in NE319/J, fired three pairs of rockets against the caique, all of which exploded in front of its bows. One of the attacks being seen in (48). All eight aircraft landed safely between 11.32 and 11.40 hours.

TUESDAY, 19 JULY 1944

Leading three other aircraft, on 19 July 1944 Wing Commander Dennis Butler and Flying Officer Roland Kemp took off in NE254/B to undertake a shipping sweep over the sea lanes in the eastern Mediterranean. The other crews were Flying Officer J.A.T. MacIntosh and Pilot Officer R.H Alderton in NE255/C, Warrant Officer W.K. Ashley and Flight Sergeant E.L. Linfield in NE472/D, and Flight Lieutenant G.G. Tuffin and Flying Officer R.A Crawford in LZ530/K. A fifth aircraft, that crewed by Flight Sergeants Stan Skippen and Jack Truscott, got airborne at the same time to act as a reserve aircraft; not needed it landed back at Gambut after being airborne for just over an hour.

At 10.50 hours a twin-masted caique was seen at anchor at position 38.35N 26.04E. All of Butler's force attacked with a pair of rockets, though these all missed. The caique was then strafed with cannon fire – it was hit and soon sank. Pictures (49) and (50) were taken during this part of the mission.

The formation then headed for Kardhamila, launching rockets at caiques in the harbour, all of which missed. Subsequent strafing resulted in at least one caique being damaged. All of the aircraft then landed back at base at 13.25 hours.

TUESDAY, 1 AUGUST 1944

The events of 1 August 1944 would prove to be costly for 252 Squadron. At 05.35 hours, four aircraft took off on an armed reconnaissance off the west coast of Greece. The Beaufighters involved were NE254/B (Squadron Leader Ian Butler and Flight Sergeant I.P. Cowl), LZ135/R (Flying Officer J.A.T. MacIntosh and Pilot Officer R.H. Alderton), NT895/H (Warrant Officer Charles Davis and Sergeant George Waller), and LZ530/K (Pilot Officer John Clark and Flight Lieutenant Edwin Young).

All four flew to Cape Skinari, before heading on to Cape Atheras. At 08.20 hours they were at the southern tip of Levas, at which point the formation split into pairs. Ian Butler and Charles Davis flew east to Meganisi and Oxia, whilst the remaining pair headed for the Kalamos Astakos area.

At 08.36 hours, Butler and Davis spotted what they thought were F-boats; both went into attack. Ian Butler was forced to break away when Charles Davis, for some unknown reason, baulked his run in to the target. Though Davis opened fire with his guns, his Beaufighter was hit and he immediately ditched. Both crew members were seen to get into a dinghy. Meanwhile, Butler's aircraft was also subjected to accurate Flak from both vessels. Badly damaged, he immediately returned to base, landing at 11.15 hours.

The other pair now headed for the dinghy and, at 08.50 hours, Flying Officer MacIntosh attacked a possible F-boat, seeing strikes from his cannon but no results from a pair of rockets. However, the Flak was once again both intense and accurate and the Beaufighter was hit along the starboard wing. John Clark now attacked with cannon, but on pulling out his aircraft was seen to be smoking and the pilot reported he was heading for Italy. Ten minutes later, the Beaufighter ditched and all that was seen afterwards was an inverted dinghy. Both crewmen were killed.

Picture (51) shows an attack made during this sortie and was brought back by one of the surviving Beaufighters.

WEDNESDAY, 6 SEPTEMBER 1944

Once again it was Wing Commander Dennis Butler who led 252 Squadron into action on 6 September 1944. Flying with the recently commissioned Pilot Officer I.P. Cowl in LZ286/A, Butler was at the head of a force of eight Beaufighters to attack enemy shipping that had been sighted earlier by a Baltimore of 459 Squadron.

The eight Beaufighters were airborne from Gambut by 10.37 hours, being escorted by four Beaufighters of 603 Squadron. At 13.14 hours, when south of Cape Sunion, a single ship was spotted. Despite 252 Squadron preparing to attack, this was abandoned as just two minutes later the original target, the convoy, was spotted. This was the 1,350-ton SS *Carola* which had left Leros the previous day. Bound for Piarus on evacuation duties, *Carola* was escorted by two Flak ships.

By this stage the Beaufighters were no longer in the best position to attack and as a result a fully coordinated strike could not be carried, the aircraft not having enough time to form up into their respective sections. Despite this, the Flak ships were attacked by both rockets and cannon fire and left smoking and damaged.

Carola was then attacked by cannon fire, the most impressive assault being by Warrant Officer J.S. Bates and Flight Sergeant S. McAughtry in NE268/Y – picture (52). Firing what was described as 'a very long burst', their aircraft can be seen in (53). The other crew to strafe *Carola* was Flying Officer Henry Deacon DFC and Pilot Officer J.D. Anderson DFM in NV243/P.

Meanwhile, 603 Squadron chased and claimed an escorting Arado Ar 196 of 2./126 as damaged. The crews of 252 Squadron reported light and inaccurate Flak, as well as a cable rocket being fired, returning with two aircraft slightly damaged. They all landed safely at 15.53 hours.

Surviving German records state that *Carola* was attacked by twelve aircraft at 12.15 hours, during which she was damaged and a few casualties received. Optimistically, the German gunners claimed to have shot down two aircraft. *Carola* limped into Piraeus and was immediately put in dry dock for repairs. On 10 October 1944, she was scuttled to act as a block ship.

SATURDAY, 9 SEPTEMBER 1944

On 9 September 1944, Wing Commander Butler and Pilot Officer Cowl, once again at the controls of LZ286/A, led seven Beaufighters on another anti-shipping strike. Airborne from Gambut at 09.33 hours, they headed towards a small convoy spotted earlier by 603 Squadron.

At 11.30 hours the Beaufighters caught up with the submarine chaser UJ-2142, which was accompanied by an armed caique, between Crete and Milos. All eight aircraft attacked twice with cannon and rockets – (54) and (55) – the crews reporting hits on UJ-2142, whilst the caique was set on fire. Again, light inaccurate Flak and rocket cables were encountered but no aircraft was damaged and they all landed safely at 13.47 hours.

The Germans later stated: 'The submarine chaser 2142 sank north of Crete after being attacked by eight planes. The loss of the vessel, so useful for the Aegean Sea, is felt very much. Details are not yet known.'

54

55

THURSDAY, 14 SEPTEMBER 1944

On 14 September, after 459 Squadron had reported seeing shipping in Paroekia Harbour on the island of Paros, eight aircraft apiece from 252 and 603 squadrons took off to undertake an offensive strike, during which pictures (56) and (57) were taken. Six of the 252 Squadron aircraft carried 25lb rockets, whilst the remaining two were equipped with 60lb rockets.

Airborne at 11.48 hours, the Beaufighters were over Paros by 14.51 hours, quickly identifying what the crews reported as a 400-ton coaster and a smaller vessel. The coaster was in fact the 260-ton minesweeper *Nordstern*.

The first to attack was Flying Officer Paddy Ward and Flight Sergeant J.G. Whitby in NV217/F, setting the smaller vessel on fire. Another three aircraft attacked this vessel with rockets and it was later reported to have sunk. The other four aircraft from 252 Squadron attacked *Nordstern*, with Flying Officer Henry Deacon and Pilot Officer J.D. Anderson in NE254/B, Warrant Officer W.K. Ashley and Flight Sergeant P.J. Gray in NT895/Q, and Warrant Officer J.S. Bates and Flight Sergeant S. McAughtry in LZ492/Q reporting to have missed with rockets. They then strafed the ship causing severe damage, noting that they left it listing. Both heavy and light Flak was encountered. Though one aircraft was damaged, everyone returned safely to land at 16.50 hours.

SUNDAY, 17 SEPTEMBER 1944

On the morning of 17 September 1944, 252 Squadron's Canadian Flying Officer Doug Reid and Flight Sergeant Ron Ray were tasked with a slightly different type of mission. Airborne from Gambut at 06.55 hours they headed out to undertake a reconnaissance of Rhodes Harbour.

They flew over the Mercantile Harbour at 1,400 feet and Flight Sergeant Ray managed to take some good photographs with a hand-held camera. The pair noted the presence of a ship moored at the West Quay – (58) and (59). The pall of thick black smoke rising from her suggested that the vessel was preparing to sail. Reid landed without incident at 10.49 hours.

TUESDAY, 19 SEPTEMBER 1944

Flying a new aircraft, NV373/A, on 19 September 1944, Wing Commander Butler and Flying Officer R.A. Crawford led seven more Beaufighters in an attack on shipping in Gaviron Harbour, Andros. Four aircraft carried 60lb rockets, the remainder 25lb rockets.

Airborne from Gambut at 12.55 hours, they arrived over the target area overland and from the north spotting a 400-600 ton coaster, later identified as the 272-ton tanker *Elli*, which was sailing from Siros to Salonika. All aircraft attacked with rockets and cannon – as depicted in pictures (60) through to (63). Warrant Officer J.S. Bates and Flight Sergeant S. McAughtry, in NE520/Z, achieved four hits with 25lb rockets on the stern, whilst Flying Officer Paddy Ward and Flight Sergeant John Whitby, in NV217/F, then hit the ship with four 60lb rockets across the stern, causing a large explosion.

Elli was soon well ablaze. Shortly afterwards explosions were seen and the stern disintegrated. As the Beaufighters broke off the attack, a further explosion was seen with smoke billowing to 2,000 feet. All aircraft landed safely at 18.08 hours.

FRIDAY, 22 SEPTEMBER 1944

At 09.48 hours on 22 September 1944, Flying Officer Paddy Ward and Flight Sergeant John Whitby took off from Gambut in NV217/F to carry out a reconnaissance of the Samos/Leros area.

Very little was seen until they approached Samos at 12.11 hours where they spotted the 1,870-ton mine-layer *Drache*, which was apparently being used to evacuate German troops, alongside the jetty at Vathi.

Almost a year to the day earlier, on 26 September 1943, Beaufighters from 252 and 227 squadrons had unsuccessfully attacked *Drache* in Syros Harbour; this time it would be different. Ward and Whitby landed back at Gambut at 14.48 hours, but, about an hour before, eight Beaufighters of 252 Squadron led by Wing Commander Dennis Butler and Flying Officer R.A. Crawford, in NV373/A, took off from Gambut. Each aircraft carried 60lb rockets. The force was accompanied by four Beaufighters from 603 Squadron which were to carry out anti-Flak cover.

At 16.17 hours, the aircraft approached Vathi overland from the south-east and attacked *Drache*, hitting it with up to fourteen rockets; Squadron Ian Butler and Flight Sergeant P.J. Gray (in NV207/I), saw four out of their eight rockets strike the target. One aircraft from 603 Squadron also managed to hit the mine-layer with a 25lb rocket. The strike was captured in pictures (64) and (65). Light and heavy Flak was encountered, albeit inaccurate, as well as cable rockets. NT901/X (Warrant Officer J.S. Bates and Flight Sergeant S. McAughtry) was hit in the tail. By the time the Beaufighters departed, *Drache* was on fire with smoke billowing from it.

The following day, a Beaufighter of 603 Squadron photographed what was left of *Drache* – which was very little as photograph (66) testifies. German records state that *Drache* was indeed set on fire, exploded and sank two hours later. Eleven crew, including her captain, Korvettenkapitän Joachim Wünning, were killed. Wünning would be awarded the Knights Cross posthumously on 22 October 1944.

SATURDAY, 23 SEPTEMBER 1944

Being used to evacuate German troops in the Aegean, the 707-ton *Orion* was initially spotted by a Baltimore of 459 Squadron sheltering in a bay at the island of Denusa, ten miles east of the island of Naxos.

On 23 September 1944, seven Beaufighters from 252 Squadron, led by Flight Lieutenant Chick Fowler and Flying Officer Roland Kemp in NV200/N, and five Beaufighters from 603 Squadron (one of which returned early) were tasked to attack it. The 252 Squadron crews were airborne from Gambut at 11.40 hours and the whole formation flew via Kaso and Santorini to Denusa.

At 14.35 hours they spotted *Orion* with its bows on the beach, as well as two barges in an adjacent cove on the south of the island. The eleven aircraft first circled Denusa before attacking from west to east – (67). Intense and accurate 20mm and 40mm anti-aircraft fire was encountered. During this barrage, Chick Fowle's Beaufighter was hit in the starboard wing, hydraulics and fuel tank (it later crash-landed at Gambut), whilst NT993/V (Warrant Officer J.S. Bates and Flight Sergeant S. McAughtry) was badly holed in the tail during what was the most successful attack of the mission.

LZ456/D, flown by Flight Sergeant Stan Skippen and Flight Sergeant Jack Truscott, was seen by a crew from 603 Squadron to be hit by tracer, jettison its rockets and break away overland. Both men were later reported killed. As the Beaufighters turned for home, a large explosion and a sheet of flame was seen inland.

All surviving aircraft landed at 16.48 hours. As there was no positive evidence that *Orion* had been destroyed, another five Beaufighters from 252 Squadron, as well as three from 603 Squadron, headed off for Denusa. The 252 Squadron crews were led by Flying Officer Paddy Ward and Flight Sergeant John Whitby in NV217/F.

They arrived over the island and discovered that *Orion* was beached and on fire. Paddy Ward attacked firing a salvo of eight 80lb rockets, of which six hit the ship. With no Flak, Ward then carried out three strafing attacks and saw smoke and steam gushing from the decks and behind the funnel. All aircraft landed unscathed at 21.30 hours.

SUNDAY, 24 SEPTEMBER 1944

Following the two attacks on *Orion* the previous day, at 07.10 hours on 24 September 1944, Australian Flying Officer F.A. McPherson of 459 Squadron got airborne from Berka in Baltimore FW609/V. With him were Flying Officer W.J. Hamilton (Navigator), Warrant Officer W.A. Fitzpatrick and Warrant Officer G.R. Mackenzie (both Wireless Operator/Air Gunners). Their reconnaissance mission covered Naxos, Paros, Denusa, Amorgos and Santorini, before they landed back at Gambut at 13.00 hours. McPherson reported that he had seen very little but on investigating the wreck of *Orion* – when image (68) was taken – was shot at by light Flak which hit an aileron. McPherson then took off from Gambut at 17.40 hours and landed back at his home base at 19.30 hours.

68

WEDNESDAY, 27 SEPTEMBER 1944

The last major mission for 252 Squadron in September 1944 took place on the afternoon of the 27th when Wing Commander Butler and Flying Officer Crawford, in NV373/A, led a formation of eight Beaufighters against shipping in Castro Harbour, Andros.

The Beaufighters were airborne at 14.25 hours and flew a route that took them to Kaso, Anaphe, Amorgos (where they were intercepted by two Supermarine Seafires), Naxos and Tenos. It was at this point that Dennis Butler went on ahead and reconnoitred Andros, spotting the 400-ton coaster *Nordmark* and another smaller ship tied up against the mole. Rejoining the rest of his formation, he led them in to the attack via the north of Andros to Gavros where they turned in and flew overland.

One of the anti-Flak aircraft was NV243/P, which, flown by Warrant Officer S.E. Legat and Flight Sergeant R.A. Paskell, exhausted all of its ammunition on both the coaster and caique before the strike force attacked with one possible hit on *Nordmark*'s bows and the jetty. A second attack was more successful, with four to six hits by rockets on the stern of *Helly* being seen. Both ships being sprayed by gunfire.

Flying Officers Stan Brunger and Ron Ramsay in LX932/T hit *Nordmark* with six rockets, causing smoke and debris to issue from the stern. Dennis Butler then made a third attack hitting *Nordmark* with a long burst of gunfire.

Pictures (69), (70) and (71) show various stages of the Beaufighters' attacks. As they left, *Nordmark* was seen to be smoking; it was confirmed sunk by 603 Squadron the following day.

On the return flight, Butler broke formation to investigate *Orion*. He found her listing badly and derelict, though he still strafed the ship as he flew overhead – (72). All aircraft landed safely at 19.50 hours.

The Germans reported the following: 'In the afternoon of 27 September, the steamer *Nordmark* and GD92 were attacked in Andros harbour by eight enemy planes flying at a low level. The *Nordmark* caught fire after being hit by a rocket and became a total loss; the GD92 was badly damaged.'

TUESDAY, 3 OCTOBER 1944

The War Diary for the Oberkommando der Marine records the following for 3 October 1943: 'At noon October 3rd, 16 enemy planes encountered a convoy of motor sailing ships near Mikronisi; two motorised sailing ships were holed and suffered casualties. Two planes were shot down.'

It was at 11.50 hours that day that four Beaufighters from 252 Squadron lifted off from Gambut, each armed with eight 25lb rockets. The crews were Canadian Flying Officer J.A.T. MacIntosh and Pilot Officer R.H. Alderton in NT895/H, Sergeants L. Armitage and R.A. Gibbons in NV207/I, Flying Officer Noel Cleggett and Pilot Officer I.P. Cowl in LX239/T, and Warrant Officer S.E. Legat and Flight Sergeant R.A. Paskell in NT901/X.

The four aircraft were to fly as an anti-Flak formation for four Beaufighters of 603 Squadron, the latter led by Wing Commander Christopher Foxley-Norris, formerly of 252 Squadron, with a further six more 603 Squadron Beaufighters acting as anti-Flak. The target was the 2,423-ton mine-layer *Zeus* which was believed to be in the Doro Channel.

After one of the 603 Squadron aircraft was forced to return with engine problems, the thirteen remaining aircraft routed via Antikythera, Melos and Keos to the Doro Channel, where they saw just five small vessels headed south. When a search failed to locate *Zeus*, the Beaufighters turned their attentions on the five small vessels, attacking at 14.25 hours – as shown in images (73), (74) and (75).

Warrant Officer Legat targeted the lead ship, described as an anti-submarine escort vessel of 250-300 tons, hitting it with gunfire on the first run. A second run started a small fire, though the four pairs of rockets fell behind the ship. For his part, Flying Officer MacIntosh attacked the fourth vessel in the line, a 200-ton lighter, hitting it with cannon fire, after which he did the same to the fifth vessel. Sergeant Armitage followed in the formation leader and attacked the lighter three times, his rockets overshooting. Finally, Flying Officer Cleggett attacked the rear caique with gunfire three times.

The lighter was left burning and abandoned, and the caique was possibly also abandoned, but still sailing on, albeit erratically. The Flak was intense, all five ships firing on the aircraft. The lead ship also fired a rocket cable.

According to the 252 Squadron Operations Record Book, all four aircraft returned safely, landing just after 17.00 hours. The same was not the case for 603 Squadron, with one of its aircraft missing, one ditching, one landing in Turkey and one belly-landing back at base. The missing crew was that of Sergeant Des Harrison and Sergeant Derek Bannister. Flying in NT895/P, the former was killed, the latter was reported. The Beaufighter that ditched was NV205/W. It was flown by Flying Officer Cas de Bounevialle and Flight Sergeant 'Gillie' Potter, both of whom were captured. New Zealander Flight Lieutenant D.G. Simpson DFC and Flight Sergeant F.G. Bunn force-landed NT964/X near Cumnovasi airfield, Turkey, at 15.43 hours, whilst it was Warrant Officer W.G. Harrison and Flying Officer Herbert Silcock, in KW346/M, who made the belly-landing,in which Silcock was injured.

73

SUNDAY, 15 OCTOBER 1944

For a change, the target given to 252 Squadron on 15 October 1944 was on land as opposed to the more customary at sea.

At 13.30 hours that day, Squadron Leader Tony Hunter and Flying Officer Roland Kemp, in NT993/V, led Flying Officer J.A.T. MacIntosh and Pilot Officer R.H. Alderton in NE479/E, Flying Officer R.W. Church and Flight Sergeant J.R. Walker in LX932/T, and Flying Officer Noel Cleggett and Pilot Officer I.P. Cowl in NV207/I to attack a building in Naxia on the island of Naxos. Each aircraft was carrying eight 60lb rockets. The building in question was where the German garrison had barricaded itself in, preventing British forces from landing on the island.

The four aircraft routed to Naxos via Gambut, Kaso, Anaphe, Amorgos and Melos. They approaching the town from the south and began to orbit. There were three British MTBs in the harbour who identified themselves and then fired smoke at the target building, this being described as a large three-storey structure with a red roof set above the harbour.

Tony Hunter led the attack making four runs, each time firing two rockets, all of which overshot. He then carried out three cannon attacks hitting the building each time. MacIntosh made his move next, completing three rocket attacks. He hit the building four times after which he strafed it. Church then undertook four attacks with rockets, five of which hit, followed by three strafing runs. By this point the building was obscured by dust so Cleggett could not see the results of his first rocket attack, whilst the rockets fired in his second pass overshot. He then strafed the building twice, after which all four aircraft headed for home, landing at 18.30 hours.

Pictures (76) and (77) show the strike underway. It is perhaps not surprising that the German garrison surrendered shortly afterwards.

76

TUESDAY, 24 OCTOBER 1944

A repeat performance of the events of 15 October was undertaken just over a week later on 24 October 1944. This time the German garrison that was to be attacked was located in a building at Calino.

Led by Flying Officer Paddy Ward and Warrant Officer E.L. Linfield, six aircraft took off at 13.10 hours. Mechanical problems soon struck Ward's Beaufighter which suffered juddering from the port engine. This had to be shut down and Paddy landed safely fifteen minutes after take-off. The lead passed to Warrant Officer S.E. Legat and Flight Sergeant R.A. Paskell in JM383/P.

The remaining five aircraft flew on to Kaso, the south-eastern tip of Kalymnos, before turning in at Linaria Bay to approach Calino down a valley. The aircraft attacked in line astern with Warrant Officer Linfield attacking first in a steep dive from 1,500 feet – picture (78). He was followed by Warrant Officer W.K. Ashley and Flight Sergeant P.J. Gray in NE479/E who managed to put a salvo of rockets into the base of the building – (79) and (80). The next to make his pass was Flying Officer R.W. Church, who was in LZ492/Q with Flight Sergeant J.R. Walker. The pair put all eight of their rockets into the building which was by now obscured by dust and smoke; similar to the view in (81).

Flying Officer Les Ferguson and Warrant Officer L. Douglas in NE520/Z attacked next, image (82), followed by Sergeants L. Armitage and R.A. Gibbons in LZ459/J who between them hit the building at least eight times.

Warrant Officer Legat then circled and attacked again with cannon, firing an accurate twelve-second burst; he then dived in again expending all of his ammunition. He was followed by Les Ferguson and Sergeant Armitage, both of whom fired long accurate bursts into the building, which was by now badly damaged, a thirty-foot hole, starting five feet from the ground and going up to the second floor, was seen.

All of the aircraft landed back safely at 17.30 hours. This sortie marked the last operational flight for the squadron in October 1944.

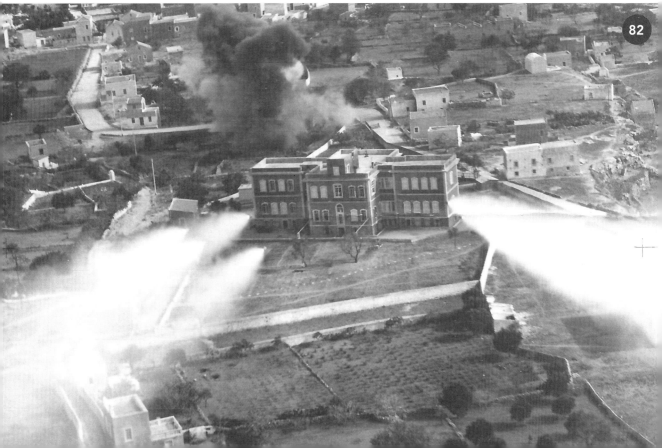

SUNDAY, 17 DECEMBER 1944

With the Germans in retreat, December 1944 saw minimal offensive action, though a number of reconnaissance flights were undertaken. On 17 December 1944, for example, Squadron Leader Tony Hunter and Flying Officer Roland Kemp, in NT993/V, and Flying Officer Doug Reid DFC, in NE520/Z (strangely, his navigator's name was not recorded, though it was probably Pilot Officer Ron Ray DFM), took off from Mersa Matruh on a shipping reconnaissance of the north coast of Crete, from Cape Sidero to Candia.

No vessels were spotted underway, though four anchored caiques were seen in a bay north of Agios Nicholaos (83), and a 60ft launch at Spinalongha after which the Beaufighters took photographs of Candia Harbour, Heraklion airfield and other locations – such as those in (84) and (85) – before landing back at base at 14.05 hours.

83

Part IV
1945

SUNDAY, 14 JANUARY 1945

At 08.55 hours on 14 January 1945, Flying Officer Paddy Ward and Flight Sergeant John Whitby, in Beaufighter NT895/H, and Flight Lieutenant Noel Cleggett and Pilot Officer I.P. Cowl, in NT995/E, took off on a shipping reconnaissance of the Dodecanese.

They first encountered a British destroyer which had no instructions for the two aircraft, after which two caiques were spotted off Patmos. These vessels, one of which can be seen in (1), hoisted the Greek flag when approached. It would then appear that the two aircraft then went sightseeing, photographing the monastery at Patmos and Stamphalia (seen beyond Patmos) – during which part of the flight pictures (2) and (3) were taken – before landing back at Mersa Matruh at 13.50 hours.

SATURDAY, 31 MARCH 1945

At 23.45 hours on 30 March 1945, Oberleutnant Karl-Heinz Stahnke of Sonderkommando Condor (part of 14 *Staffel/Transportgeschwader* 4), and who had been awarded the *Eichenlaub* to his *Ritterkreuz* three days before, took off from Wiener Neustadt in Focke-Wulf Fw 200 Condor coded G6+AY.

Stahnke's destination was Calato in Rhodes, where he arrived just before dawn on 31 March. Having landed, the Condor was spotted, together with a He 111 and a Ju 52, by an Allied photo-reconnaissance aircraft. Led by Squadron Leader Tony Hunter, six of 252 Squadron's Beaufighters, which were then based at Hassani in Greece, were tasked to try and destroy the aircraft, taking off at 14.50 hours.

This was not the first time, however, that 252 Squadron had gone after Stahnke's Condor whilst it was at Calato. On 17 March 1945, Flying Officer Doug Reid DFM and Flying Officer Ron Ray DFM carried out a first light recce looking for the Fw 200 which had arrived two days earlier. The pair failed to locate the Condor, though it had been there, Stahnke not taking off for Austria until the following day.

Returning to the events of 31 March, on arriving over Calato in two formations of three, the Beaufighter crews saw nothing, so promptly attacked buildings on the airfield with cannon, experiencing moderate to light Flak in return (interspersed with the occasional heavy Flak burst). This damaged the tail of Flying Officer Joe Underwood's Beaufighter, whilst Flight Sergeant

L.G. Armitage's aircraft was hit in the nose and Flying Officer's Bill Escreet's 'plane suffered a burst undercarriage tyre.

Despite this, all six landed safely back at Hassani. On developing camera gun film taken by Flying Officer Doug Reid, to everyone's great annoyance the Condor could be seen cleverly camouflaged under olive trees – picture (4).

Stahnke took off that evening. At the end of the war, the Allies discovered G6+FY, together with its pilot, Oberfeldwebel Adalbert Schaffranek, and his crew, at Calato, the German crew having arrived there on 3 May 1945.

FRIDAY, 4 MAY 1945

With the end the war in Europe just a few days away, the beginning of May 1945 would, for obvious reasons, see 252 Squadron flying just two operational sorties and both were against the four gun coastal defence battery at Melos.

On 4 May 1945, eight aircraft led by the Commanding Officer, Squadron Leader Tony Hunter, and Flying Officer Doug Holden, who were in NV615/V, took off from Hassani at 14.55 hours. The Beaufighters attacked the guns in two waves of four, diving down from 2,400 feet to 800 feet with each aircraft singling out a specific gun. Five aircraft fired salvoes of eight rockets, one fired a pair only, whilst Flight Sergeant L.G. Armitage and Flight Sergeant R.A. Gibbons, in NT995/E, failed to fire at all. It is believed that Tony Hunter got a direct hit on the mid-port gun but the other pilots over or under shot.

The first photograph, (5), shows the attack made by Squadron Leader Noel Cleggett and Flying Officer I.P. Cowl in NV147/C; the remaining two, (6) and (7), were taken by Flying Officer Paddy Ward and Pilot Officer John Whitby in NV373/A. Intense light Flak was encountered, with NT966/B (Flying Officer Henry Deacon DFC and Flying Officer J.D. Anderson DFM) being hit in the tail and NT995/E (Flight Sergeants L.G. Armitage and R.A. Gibbons) being damaged in the wing root, tail and wing tip. All eight aircraft returned safely, landing at 1814 hours. It is interesting to note that two aircraft (NE254/I and NV485/N) patrolled off Melos as standby aircraft, though no mention is made of their crew in the Operations Record Book.

5

SATURDAY, 5 MAY 1945

For its last operational sortie of the war in Europe, the aircraft of 252 Squadron returned to Melos. The force of nine Beaufighters was once again led by Squadron Leader Tony Hunter who, with Flying Officer Roy Child as his navigator, was at the controls of the same aircraft as the previous day.

Taking off from Hassani between 14.47 and 14.50 hours, each aircraft was armed with eight rockets. As before they attacked in two waves, flying in from east to west, with the ninth aircraft following the second wave.

It was judged that Flying Officer Ron Faulkner and Flying Officer R.H. Williams, in NV373/V, scored a direct hit on the mid-right gun – as pictures (8) and (9) show. The third photograph, (10), was taken by Flying Officer Paddy Ward and Pilot Officer John Whitby in NV147/C. It was also noted that Flight Sergeant L.G. Armitage and Flight Sergeant R.A. Gibbons, in NT995/E, probably scored a direct hit on the extreme left gun, this aircraft also being hit in the nose by flying debris. The last two photographs, (11) and (12), depict Armitage's attack.

All aircraft had landed by 16.31 hours. The war for 252 Squadron was finally over.

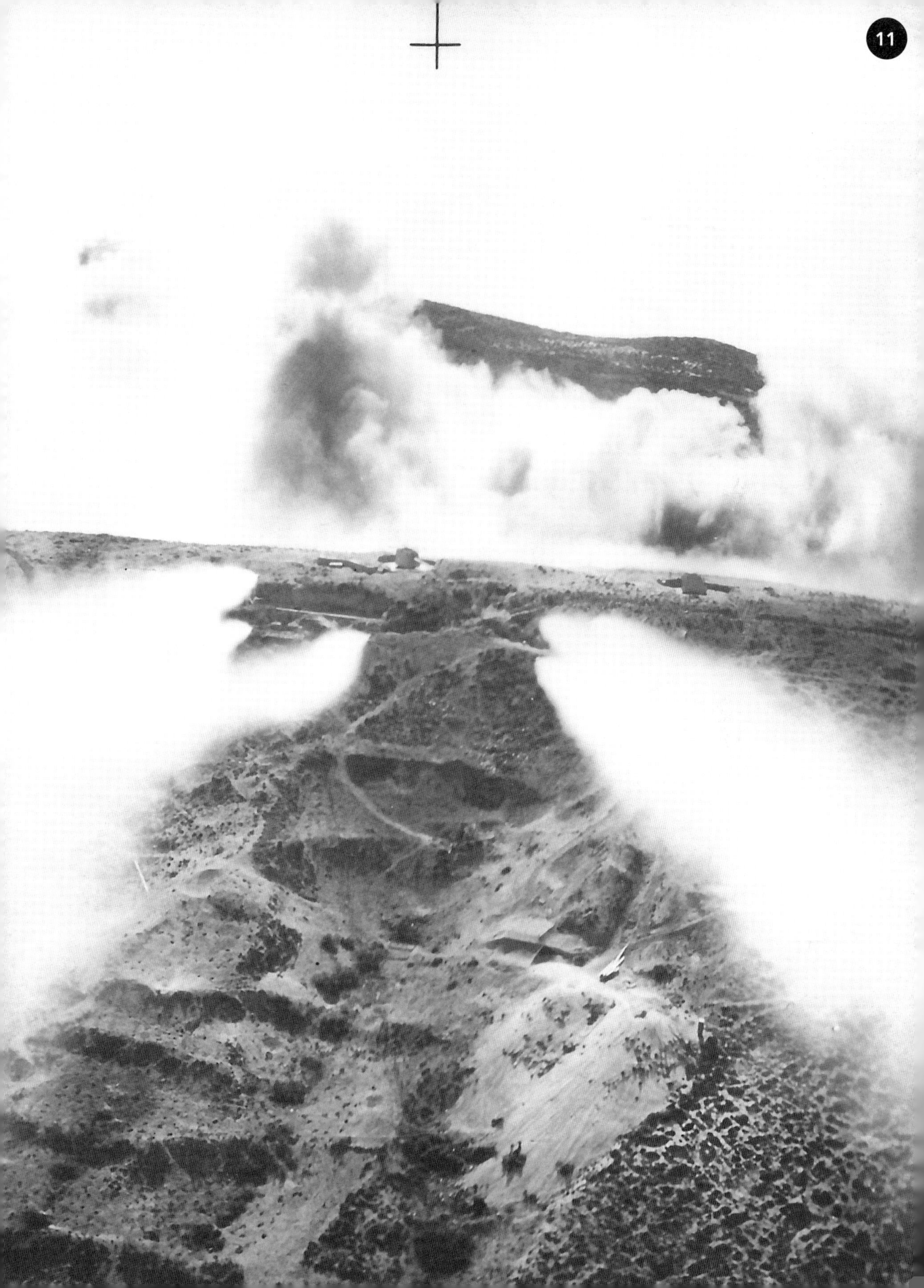